Calel

Calel

A MEMOIR OF MY
GREEK MOTHER

Cally Berryman, PhD

Published in Australia by
Marble Media
Email: callyberryman@hotmail.com
Website: Callyberryman.com

First published in Australia 2018

National Library of Australia Cataloguing –in –
Publication entry
Berryman, Cally
Calel. A Memoir of My Greek Mother
ISBN: 978-0-6482851-0-6

Cover layout and design by graphic designer Nelly

About the author

Cally Berryman, PhD, was born in Lesvos, Greece. She came to Australia with her mother and father and two older brothers in 1952.

Cally is a registered nurse and has been employed in a variety of areas including: counsellor, drug and alcohol detox, acute medical and surgical, community, and an academic in two universities.

Cally has written two novels:

The Accidental Gambler (Fiction)

Calel A Memoir of My Greek Mother (Nonfiction)

She is currently writing a third Novel.

Acknowledgments

In loving gratitude to my wonderful Mother and Father and brothers John and Jim who came to Australia in 1952 with empty pockets but large dreams.

Contents

PART 3
Through the eyes of an adult – the beginning of the adventure

PART 4
Brother and sister reunited

PART 5
Mother dies

PART 6
Seeing the world through older woman's eyes. Return to Mytilene, 2009

Prologue

When our family lived in Springvale, my Mother owned a textured rug of black and yellow. It had interlocking geometric shapes, was oblong in size and had black tassels around its edges. My Great Grandmother made the rug. She washed, carded, and spun the wool that was shorn from her own sheep. The yarn was coloured by mineral and vegetable dyes, then spun by a hand spindle and woven using a wooden loom.

The rug became part of my grandmother's dowry, which was handed down to my mother.

This small woven rug had a life of its own, moving around our home. Sometimes it was found draped over the sewing machine; another day arranged at the back of the divan in the lounge. It would disappear into the linen press for weeks and then appear on the coffee table.

"Calel," Mother said. This was her pet name for me when she was happy with me.

"This is the one piece of Mytilene that I still possess."

I never knew the significance of that statement until I was older.

PART 1

A child's view of the world

CHAPTER 1

We did not come to Australia for this

Springvale

1956

It was the end of a warm spring day, the perfume of honeysuckle filtering through the open window. Taffy, our dog, started barking, yelping and making intense growling noises outside. Loud shouts came from the laundry room; they were followed by the sound of things crashing. I rushed to the laundry and yanked the door open.

To my horror, Father had my brother John by the scruff of his shirt.

"Quick, go next door and ask the neighbours to call the police," John said, his voice panicked. "Dad has gone mad."

He struggled to get up.

"Yes, call the police," Father said, his voice showing no emotion. "I want to report the death of my son."

Turning to John, he shouted in Greek, "We

didn't come to Australia for this, for you to become a criminal."

Father twisted John's shirt and tried to strike John with his other hand.

John blocked his hand, fell and was jammed in the corner of the laundry.

Father's voice grew icy.

"We came to Australia for a better life...instead, you are friends with boys who are thieves."

"Dad, it's not like that," said John.

He backed off and overturned two metal soaking buckets.

A river of water, soapy football shorts, and jumpers oozed onto the green and white linoleum floor and sloshed all over John. He tried to get up, knocking winter coats from the hooks above him.

"I would rather kill you now than see you waste your life," Father said.

He straightened up and walked to the kitchen. He rummaged in the cutlery drawer, found a blunt bread and butter knife. He returned to John, who was trying to sit up; his clothes soaking wet, coats covering his feet.

"Dad..." cried John, his voice shrill.

I screamed.

Mother came into the room and shrieked in Greek "Stop Michael...stop."

Father leaned over John with the bread and butter knife in his hand, aimed at John's heart.

"Do you want to be a criminal or do you want to go to school?"

"School..." John croaked, pushing the knife away. "School...I promise."

I couldn't be sure if my Father was bluffing or not. I was eight and clung tightly to my father's back, trying with all my strength to pull him away from John.

"Don't kill John. Don't kill John," I shouted.

Our dog barked furiously outside.

"Dad." I screeched. "He said school...he said school."

Father heard my panic-stricken voice. He turned looking at me. Tears welled up in his eyes.

His voice was inaudible.

Father threw the bread and butter knife on the linoleum floor. His head bowed, tears run down his face. He opened the back door to the yard.

The dog saw Father and circled, still barking.

I had never seen Father cry; neither had John.

We gaped at each other, stunned, unnerved.

I grabbed John's arm to help him up as water dripped off his clothes.

Took the bread and butter knife and hurled it in the sink.

"God help us!" cried Mother. She pounded her fists on her head.

~

Earlier that day, Father on his way home from an early shift at work, walked from the station and saw puffs of tobacco smoke coming from the long grass. He recognised John's voice and surprised John and his friend Sam. They had both wagged school. Sam disappeared as soon as he saw Father.

"What's going on? Why aren't you in school?" Father asked John.

John tried to scramble into the bushes. Father grabbed him by the trousers and dragged him home. His anger rose the more John struggled.

~

Everyone knew Sam's father had spent time in jail. Young Sam had already been in juvenile detention for stealing cars. I knew John and Sam often wagged school. My brother was thrilled with Sam's friendship and crazy ways.

We had been in Australia for two years. John had found the transition from being a high achieving student in Mytilene, now two levels below his academic grade, difficult and embarrassing. He hated school. Sam offered him an escape.

~

The house fell silent. Father stayed in the vegetable garden, digging and turning the soil until dark. John muttered that he had plans to run away from home.

My other brother Jim comforted Mother, who

was still upset. I tightly held my doll, Christine, and kept an eye on Father in the garden.

John made a show of retrieving his treasured comics that were hidden under his mattress. He burnt them in the incinerator.

"Call your father for dinner," Mother said, her voice brittle.

"Dinner," I said.

I pulled at Father's sleeve. It was dark, the stars were out. A large full moon shone brightly.

"My little girl," he said. He stopped digging and hugged me.

"Make sure you study hard and be the best you can be."

"I promise," I said.

Mother had cooked Father's favourite meal of tender lamb casserole and beans. The delicious aroma hung in the tiny kitchen. A red and white checked tablecloth spread over the small oblong table. A cane basket held cut bread. The five of us sat cramped together. Father sat at the far end of the table; John and Jim on the other side next to each other. Mother on the other side close to the gas stove and metal sink. I was in my usual spot at the other end of the table.

"Thank you for the food we are about to eat," said Father; he hesitated. "Thank you for my family. Thank you for keeping us safe today."

Father always said grace before meals.

"Amen," we said together.

I looked at John. He was avoiding Father's gaze, had his head down eating. Jim glanced at me and shrugged his shoulders. Mother ate in silence, as did Father. I tried to find a bridge, a middle ground to fix things and restore the peace between John and Father.

"Lovely meal, Mum," I said in Greek.

Mother ignored me.

"Did you have a nice day at work today?" I said to Father. He did not answer.

"I learned to play Greensleeves on my recorder during music class," I said.

"Shut up Cally," said Jim.

And I did.

"Let me do the dishes," I said at the end of the meal. I carefully stacked the dishes, then ran the wire mesh holder with scraps of velvet soap under the hot water until the soap made a bubble bath in the sink. Normally I hated doing the dishes and avoided it all costs. The soapy mess flooded the sink and dripped down to the floor.

"I will take over now," said Mother, pushing me away from the sink.

Later that evening, Sam came to our house looking for John. Father stood under the porch light and said through clenched teeth.

"Never, do you hear me...never, come near my son again."

Sam, a thin, reedy redhead, looked between Father and John. He was going to argue but saw

John shake his head at him. Sam scampered down the porch steps.

I never knew if John kept a secret friendship going with Sam or not. But, John made a show of doing his homework at the kitchen table whenever Father came home.

~

My family expressed themselves loudly, maybe it was the European way, but it frightened me. In my heart, I wished we were as other families that appeared quiet and orderly and no shouting.

Friend Rosy's family had the hallmarks of peacefulness. I never heard arguments between her father and mother. In our home, Father and Mother seemed to endlessly shout and argue among themselves. And my brothers bickered constantly.

I often held my hands over my ears, fearful of loud shouting and threats to leave or worse. I have an image of clinging onto both parents, fearful one would leave forever. Mother seemed to be always sobbing, Father often shouting.

My parents loved each other dearly, but the lack of money, day-to-day stresses, and dislocation in a strange land without a wider family or support created conflict.

Mother told me she had been reluctant to leave Lesvos and migrate to Australia because of Father's dream. The reality was nothing as promised. No land of milk and honey. Instead, Mother experienced poverty and isolation. It had been very difficult for Father to find employment in his occupation as an accountant as his qualifications were not recognised in Australia. In those days, Australia only wanted migrants to work in factories. Father obtained a job at the General Motor Holden plant at Fisherman's Bend on the assembly line. The shift work was dirty and dangerous and difficult for a man used to using his brain not his hands. At one stage, he sustained damage to his right hand, getting it caught in the machinery, requiring an operation. Crying in pain, his hand bound with bandages, Father would still go to work. After some time, he found a job as a letter sorter at the city Post Office.

When we shifted into the Springvale house, it was devoid of furniture. In the beginning, we slept on the bare boards in the lounge huddled in front of the open fire. Later beds and table and chairs were bought on credit.

Despite the downturn of circumstances from what it had been in Lesvos, Father envisioned enormous possibilities for his family in Australia and remained positive.

"Things will get better soon," he said to Mother, giving her a hug. "We have to learn to be patient."

"I hate Australia; I want to go back home to Lesvos," Mother said.

"You cannot go back. This is your country now," Father said.

"I want to go back to Lesvos to see my mother," Mother said.

Mother cried every time a letter arrived from Lesvos. We would sit at the kitchen table and she would read and reread the letters to me.

"Calel," she said. "I want you to promise me that we will return to Lesvos together."

"Yes," I said, never imagining such a trip.

She felt homesick and isolated. The rest of the family had become embedded into the Australian culture of work and school. But Mother had not. It must have been lonely for her; we children drifted away from her and from our Greek culture and heritage in an effort to belong to friends. To my shame, I remembered telling Mother, "Speak English" when I was with my friends and she spoke to us in Greek.

Father wanted us to be real Australians; we attended the Church of England. John, Jim, and I joined Sunday school. Father was popular with the local church community. Mother helped with the church flowers. She told me she missed the chanting, the incense, and vibrancy of the Greek Church.

There were no Greek churches near us at the time. But each Easter, we attended the packed Greek Church in Melbourne City. One year, a man fainted in the crowded church; I remember my Father brought him a glass of water and looked after him until he was all right.

Few Greek families lived in the Springvale district and none in the Returned Soldiers' area where we lived. The housing region of simple weatherboard homes housed returned soldiers and their families. These men returned from the World War II changed and with visible and nonvisible battle scars. Some drank heavily to forget the demons and nightmares from distant wars.

In the weatherboard house opposite our home lived a returned soldier who piled his daily empty beer bottles into a type of shrine in the backyard. We could hear his drunken swearing from our home and it became a nightly occurrence. I watched him stagger home each day holding a cardboard box full of beer.

Years later, when working as a nurse at The Alfred Hospital, while I waited in line at the canteen for lunch, one of this man's daughters recognised me and tapped me on the shoulder.

"Did you live on the corner of Ericksen Street in Springvale?" she asked.

"Yes," I said.

The man's daughter said she had been ashamed of her family and their drinking and envied my family.

"Your father and mother never drank. You gave us vegetables from your garden and eggs." She looked down.

"My brother now has an alcoholic brain injury

and cannot tie his shoelaces. He is only thirty-five and is in an institution."

I held my breath.

"As soon as I could I escaped from home. My brother and parents ended up as alcoholics," She shook her head.

"I was so afraid that I would be an alcoholic if I stayed at home."

She looked me in the eye. "You were so lucky," she said. "I am afraid to have any children in case I carry the family alcohol gene."

I didn't know what to say. For a split moment, I turned my head to reply to a colleague who was speaking to me.

When I turned back, she was gone.

There were those in Ericksen Street who led sober lives; most people tended to keep to themselves in those days.

Our weatherboard house on the corner of Ericksen Street may have been full of conflict, but the garden shone under both parents' loving attention. The front yard was ablaze with red roses and hydrangeas. The backyard had carefully arranged rows of potatoes, beans, tomatoes, lettuce, and cucumbers which we shared with neighbours. And chickens pecked at the back.

John and Jim shared one bedroom. Sometimes they hated each other and argued. Other times they got on well. They were opposite in nature. John the optimist, gregarious, had many friends. Jim was quieter, neat, and introverted. He was the closest to Mother and talented at art and drawing. She called Jim her 'Golden Boy.'

John liked to destabilise his brother.

Jim, in turn, laid complex traps to catch John messing up his comics and treasured collections.

"You have been messing around in my comic pile," said Jim.

John laughed, "Prove it."

Jim would show the trap he had set; several long strands of hair draped over his comics; these were now scattered on the ground.

CHAPTER 2

Father's accident

Springvale

November 1956

"Are you Mrs Evangelou, wife of Michael Evangelou?" the stranger asked.

It was dark outside; he was illuminated against the light of the front porch. Rain dripped from his cap, a tall man, his head almost touched the porch light. Another man stood behind him.

He repeated the question. "Are you Mrs Evangelou, wife of Michael Evangelou?"

Mother appeared dazed, stared intently at the two men in navy blue uniform at the door.

"Calel," she said to me in Greek, "What did he say?"

My heart beat faster; I held my breath standing next to Mother. Father had been late home from work. I waited with her to keep her company. She had been anxious all night, every few minutes looking up from her sewing listening for his footsteps.

Mother had been sewing a coat for me and still held the sleeve of the blue wool in her hand. A sewing needle with navy blue thread was pinned hastily to her green cardigan. She still had the thimble on her finger.

Brothers John and Jim were asleep.

The two police officers looked at me, pigtailed, nine years old, wearing a red, handmade woollen dressing gown.

"Can we come in?"

I nodded yes.

The lounge lights flicked on; the chairs scrapped as they sat. Their voices boomed and echoed off the walls. The smell of wet wool filled the small lounge room. They sat awkwardly on the edge of the chairs, both holding their caps.

No one spoke.

The taller man cleared his throat.

Mother's eyes grew wild, darting back and forth at the men.

The taller one said softly, "Mrs Evangelou, I guess you understand we are police officers. We have just attended a motor vehicle accident near your home."

The shorter police officer put Father's brown Galston work bag on the floor.

Silence.

I translated.

Mother twisted the blue woollen sleeve in her hands and looked sorrowfully at the men.

"We are sorry to tell you," the taller man stopped and swallowed. "Your husband was hit by a car on his way home from work tonight. He must have been on the late train and the accident occurred when he crossed the road."

A blast of chill air covered my heart, please...please no...

The police officer turned to look at me to continue.

I could not speak. Tears ran down my face.

Mother looked at me hard, her voice thin.

"What Calel...what...?"

I whispered his words to her in Greek.

"He has been taken by ambulance to The Alfred Hospital and is badly injured. He is critically ill," said the policeman.

"Do you understand the words critically ill?" he said to me.

I shook my head. I was too sick with fear, sick with the words. Bile rose in my mouth making me want to vomit.

"Very sick. Your father may die."

The taller one shifted his navy blue police officer's hat awkwardly in his hand. He glanced at his clipboard. His tall frame doubled up on the chair. The other police officer remained silent.

I translated for Mother.

"God, my God!" Mother screamed in Greek.

I put my hands over my ears.

Hearing Mother's guttural cries, John and Jim burst into the room in their striped pyjamas.

The police officer passed Father's brown bag to John. It had dried blood on the handle.

I saw it.

We all saw the blood and we all knew that something terrible had happened to Father.

He solemnly handed Mother a folded magazine Father had been carrying. There was a splodge of dried, dark blood on the pages obliterating the words.

Both police officers looked uncomfortable.

Mother's crying grew louder. She pounded her fists to her head. I tried to hold her hands. John and Jim were quiet.

Felt myself mentally drifting onto the ceiling, trying to get away.

"Which hospital did you say? When can we see our father?" John asked.

"Is there anyone we can ring for you? Do you have any family? Can we bring anyone to help you?" The taller policeman asked. His face wrinkled with concern.

"There is no one, just us here," said John.

"We have no phone, no relatives in Australia."

"Cally, go and make us all a cup of tea," John said to me calling me by my Australian name. He wanted to protect me.

I ran the water into the kettle, searched for the matches to light the gas, and lifted the kettle onto the gas. I fumbled for the teapot, cups, and tea. I heard John offer the police officers tea; they refused, as they said they had to keep going because they were still on duty.

I heard Mother's anguished cries rise and then become quieter, a hum of male voices, and my brothers asking questions. Made the tea, but the milk had soured. I threw the milk in the sink. I brought the tray with cups of black tea. Held the tray for a long time not sure what to do. After a time, I placed the tray noiselessly on the table.

I took one cup of tea of black tea to my mother and placed her hands around the cup. My brothers stood in their pyjamas next to the police officers. The taller officer wrote 'Alfred Hospital Commercial Road Prahran' on a scrap of paper and handed it to John.

One police officer looked at his watch and nodded to the other. They stood up, John opened the front door, and they left.

We stared, numb and unable to move as the police banged down the steps and into the darkness. Saw the police car door lights turn on inside the police car. The headlights came on, and we gaped as they drove away. The night's darkness filled the space where the car had been. It had rained; condensation hung over the lounge room window, smeary and opaque.

Mother's hands shook as she lit a small candle that floated in a small dish of oil in front of the dark green and gold icon of St George killing a dragon. It stood on a small table as a sacred space in a corner of my parent's bedroom. Mother prayed softly for Father's life to be spared. We all prayed and crossed ourselves. The oil and burnt match smell lingered. The light of the small candle bobbed and floated on the small oil dish, reflecting a powerful St George with a huge sabre.

Mother crossed herself repeatedly.

We said The Lord's Prayer in English.

"Please look after our Father and make him well," we said again and again, as if just saying the words had magic powers to make things right.

The dark shadows of our bodies danced behind us in the candlelight.

I found my doll Christine and hugged her tight. Father had bought me the toy the year before. We huddled together on the dark maroon divan in the lounge room. There were a few pieces of furniture in the lounge room; a small divan, a runner of carpet on bare wooden boards. A few chairs and a table. We had no curtains, sheets hung over the windows.

The room felt empty and cold.

John lit the fire. It crackled, a warm glow enveloped the room, smoke drifted up the chimney. Mother was still in her dress and green cardigan, John and Jim in pyjamas, and me in my dressing gown.

I hugged Christine tightly.

Jim dragged the blue blanket from his bed, spread it out over us. We bunched up close. I shivered with shock and leaned against my mother, then jumped when pricked by the needle secured on her cardigan.

The four of us waited until the black sky became grey and then pink. Birds chirped to each other. It stopped raining. Cars drove up and down the road outside swishing in the puddles.

Mother said something to John, and he opened Father's brown bag. He located his pay packet. He handed it to my mother who stood frozen, afraid to open its contents.

When the morning came, Mother washed my face and brushed my hair, combing it into two thick plaits.

"Calel, be a good girl," she said softly.

"Pray for your Father. Be like an angel for him."

I nodded.

She kissed me and held me tightly. I could taste the salt of her tears.

Mother cut thick bread slices, added tasty cheese, and wrapped it in wax paper. She covered it with a checked cloth, placed it in her bag.

She made the same for Jim and me. Jim had to stay with me. In those days, young children were not allowed in Intensive Care wards.

Mother pulled on her navy coat, wrapped a dark blue scarf around her face. She stepped down the porch, John beside her, stretching himself trying to look tall. They walked the forty minutes to Springvale railway station, caught the first train to Flinders Street, then a tram to Prahran and The Alfred Hospital. They made the journey to my Father's comatose body at the Alfred Hospital where they stayed for the next three days.

Father never regained consciousness and died three days later from massive head injuries.

CHAPTER 3

Trips to the cemetery

Springvale

1956 onwards

Each Sunday, Mother and I caught the bus from the end of Ericksen Street to the Springvale highway. Mother carried a brown basket. We trudged for thirty minutes to the Springvale cemetery. Once inside the massive wrought iron gates, we kept going for another fifteen minutes to locate the Armed Forces Memorial.

Usually, I wore my Sunday best clothes: best cotton, blue dress with white buttons and navy cardigan. I stopped to admire the roses and camellias by the small artificial stream.

The Armed Forces memorial was neatly set out in rows; each soldier allocated a bronze and concrete memorial plaque placed next to red and white rose bushes. The plaques identified young men killed in a variety of wars in faraway places. There was an Australian flag and elaborate marching, and band services played on Anzac Day.

The Last Post bugle call made me shiver; it was so beautiful.

"In the going down of the sun...we will remember them."

I always remembered my Father; he was always in my thoughts and dreams.

He was buried in the adjoining lawn cemetery which was situated next to the Armed Forces Memorial. His lawn grave was forty walking paces from the concrete seat near the road to the old gum tree in Row T. Usually, I counted the steps. It was easy to miss the plaque. It seemed that each time we came there were more and more graves.

Soon, I would be shaking with anxiety, dreading what was to come. I knew what to expect.

Before I finished counting the paces to Father's grave, Mother would start crying.

Silently we unpacked the basket together. It held a thermos of tea, flowers, and cleaning products. My job was to clean the bronze plaque with Silvo until it shone, then carefully trim the bits of lawn that stuck out around the plaque using a small pair of nail scissors.

Mother arranged the pink carnations from our garden around the plaque. The carnations were special. Father had planted them the year before and they bloomed all year around.

By now, Mother's grief was unstoppable. It burst out of her. Her head bent on the lawn next to the grave and she stamped the grass with her fists.

"I never wanted to come to Australia and you died and left me here and I cannot go back home."

Her voice rose louder and became hysterical until she was emptied. “Why did you leave us?” she asked.

Mother’s face tear-stained, her hair in disarray, would put her hands over her face. Then gathering some internal energy would start crying again.

Usually, I stood a few paces behind repeatedly reciting the Lord’s Prayer. I think it created a talisman; a sheet of comforting words so I would not fall into her abyss of grief.

I felt helpless and could not help her.

Sometimes I edged along the row of graves, reading the names of people who had died, every so often peering around to see if anyone could hear and see us.

After Mother stopped crying, we opened the flask of tea and drank a cup each. Mother would rearrange the flowers again, so they were perfect around the plaque.

“Bless and keep our beloved Father,” we said and stood silent.

I looked at the sky and wondered where Father was and why he had to leave us. If he could see us and see how much we needed him he might come back. He had been to war and came back safe. But in Australia, he died.

We slowly meandered out of the cemetery. Mother kept crossing herself and looking upwards on the way back home. The Sunday bus services finished at 2 p.m. If we missed the last bus, it would take us more than an hour to trek home.

Neither of us spoke.

When we returned home, Mother lay on her bed and stared at the ceiling.

I would go outside, sit on the back step with my face buried in my skirt. I was nine years old and had no idea what to do. I missed Father so much it burned a hole inside of me but felt I could not say anything as Mother was struggling so much.

"Where are you Father? Please come back," I whispered.

I knew he was not at the cemetery.

CHAPTER 4

Olympic games

Melbourne

1956

There were four of us cramped on the lounge seat. The walls were covered in gold and white wallpaper. The white Venetian blinds closed. The room was dark except for the glow of a small side lamp. We fidgeted, rearranging ourselves, stood and sat. Coughed and sniffled.

Mother, John, Jim, and I were squashed on the green velvet lounge. I kept trying to squeeze in so as not to fall off, but my brothers had hogged most of the space. Mr and Mrs Armstrong were in their two big armchairs. Their son Jeffery and Mr and Mrs Keats and their daughter Ann sat on the kitchen chairs. The air smelt of Brylcreem; the men used it to slick their hair, now and then a waft of Tweed perfume. All of us dressed in our good clothes, polished shoes, hair combed, women in high heels and lipstick.

Everyone stared at the blue light of the television as it flickered from its mysterious wooden box in the corner of the room.

Our neighbour, Mrs Armstrong, had invited our family and three other neighbours to watch the 1956 Olympic Games on her new television.

"Cold War violence has erupted at the Olympic Games," said the television commentator, his voice stricken with emotion.

"A fierce water polo match between Hungary and Russia has just ended in a frightening scene. A Russian player had punched a Hungarian player in the eye."

We sucked in our breaths and cries of "Oh no!" filled the lounge room.

We glued our eyes to the TV, watching as angry spectators jumped on the concourse near the pool. The crowd shook their fists, shouting abuse and spitting at the Russians.

"It's a riot. Where are the police?" asked Mr Armstrong.

Eventually, the police appeared at the concourse and held the crowd back forcibly. The people who had remained in the galleries of the stands roared. They started shouting and stomping their feet and throwing arms in the air.

The announcer kept asking for calm, repeating: "People not connected to the water polo kindly leave the concourse."

During the match, both teams had exchanged kicks and punches. The referee had previously ordered three Russians and two Hungarians players out of the water. The galleries were packed with predominately Hungarian migrants, who cheered each goal for their countrymen. Any Russian attempt drew groans and jeers.

Valentine Prokopov of Russia swam up to Ervin Zador of Hungary and punched him in the eye while the ball was in the other end of the pool. Zador could be seen climbing defiantly out of the pool, blood streaming down his face from the cut above his eye. Flashes from hundreds of cameras filled the background. The spectators went wild. They shouted, stomped and jeered. Hungarian officials jumped their barrier and shook their fists at the Russian. The Russian team stood at the shallow end of the pool with heads bowed.

The announcer said, “Hungary has won the match by four goals to Russia’s nil.” Uproar followed, the spectators screamed and clapped, jumped to their feet as one. The Russian team left the pool amid jeers and hoots trailing after them.

“It’s not water polo out there. It’s boxing in the water,” said the television commentator, his voice hysterical.

He repeated the score amid fresh applause and shouting.

“We are going to a commercial break,” he said with audible relief.

The Cold War tensions between Russia and Hungary had been played out in front of us and it placed Australia in the political arena. The news of the event was relayed on media networks throughout the world. Australia had previously been largely isolated from European political issues. The Russian invasion of Hungary and the Hungarian rebellion barely rated a mention in the papers.

From the safety of the leafy street in Springvale, we made comments and were angered by the unfairness of the blow by the Russian to the Hungarian.

The 1956 Olympics in Melbourne was the first to be staged in the Southern Hemisphere. It had been mired in political controversy from the start. Many of the formal Olympic Committee members had been sceptical that Melbourne would be the appropriate place for the Olympics. There had been bickering over finances by politicians. Egypt, Iraq, and Lebanon announced they would not participate in the Games due to the Suez Canal crisis. Egypt had been invaded by Israel, the United Kingdom, and France in response to Egypt nationalising the Suez Canal. The Soviet Union had previously crushed a Hungarian revolution. When the Soviets said they were attending, it led to the withdrawal of the Netherlands, Spain, and Switzerland from the Games.

Two weeks before the 22 November 1956 Olympic Games opening, the People's Republic of China boycotted the event. But once things were underway, the Olympic Games appeared to go smoothly and were called the 'Friendly Games.'

Television was rolled out in Melbourne at the

time of the Games, but few people could afford a television.

Back in Springvale, the lights in the lounge room sprung on. We blinked.

"Time for supper," Mrs Armstrong said and clapped her hands.

She was a small round woman with a booming voice, her husband thin and tall and quiet.

Each woman had bought a plate of food. The wooden sideboard laden with sandwiches, meringues with cream filling and passion fruit topping, thick slices of bread covered in hundreds and thousands of sweets.

The room buzzed with conversation: "so unfair" and "terrible" and "I can't believe it." Jeffery, tall like his father, passed around a plate of sandwiches. Mr Armstrong distributed cups of hot cocoa from a tray.

"Do you take sugar?" he asked.

My father had been killed by a driver in a car accident a few weeks earlier. Our family had been shattered and rudderless with no family near us.

The kindness of neighbours and friends sustained us.

Despite the death of my Father, John and Jim begged Mother to see the Olympic City displays in Melbourne city.

“Please Mother, this is a once-in-a-lifetime event,” said John.

“We need to write about it for school,” said Jim.

They pleaded with Mother for days.

“No, I cannot give permission,” she said.

She wanted to stay home in the dark house and cry, as she did every day.

My brothers wanted to see the city. But she would not let the boys go by themselves, too fearful that they too would be lost to her.

“All right,” she said one day, as though resigned to life.

The four of us walked to the station; we were a quiet group walking close together. Mother wore the same mourning clothes she wore every day since Father’s death; black skirt, black jumper, black stockings, and shoes. A navy scarf covered her head, her face downturned.

The family used the shortcut to Westall station, through the long grass, past the rows of old quince trees that had been on someone’s property and now belonged to the Victorian railways. The quinces were not ripe yet. When they were ready, we brought them home hidden under our jumpers. Mother would stew the quinces; we would eat them with sugar and cream to hide the tartness.

As usual John and Jim bickered, their preferred line of communication.

"I did not," said John.

"Yes, you did," said Jim.

I tiptoed through the grass, watching for snakes. John and Jim told me terrifying stories of snakes that hid in the long grass and slithered and attacked you for no reason. I looked down at the grass, careful not to step on any snakes.

We caught the train from the new station, Westall, and travelled to Flinders Street station. The train was packed with laughing, shouting families. I kept glancing at Mother. She stared at her hands folded on her lap. My brothers kept pushing and shoving each other.

Flinders Street station was festooned with Olympic symbols, giant circles intertwined. Flags of every nationality fluttered in the streets. We poured out of Flinders Street station, as the clocks at St Paul's cathedral rang loudly. Men women and children were packed together in the streets. They shouted, screamed, pushed and shoved. Police on horseback blew whistles and urged everyone to "stay calm."

Trams rattled past, packed with people. Our family joined a river of people moving in the same direction down Swanston Street. Families with babies in prams moved as one. The crowd pushed us to Bourke Street.

Myer and other stores had special Olympic

Games displays in their windows. People queued to view the colourful window displays. One Myer window had a television switched on to the day's Olympic events, people milled around.

I stood on tiptoes to see, Mother clung tightly to my hand.

"Can I have your autograph?" a boy asked a tall black man. The boy's autograph book and pencil held up high.

CHAPTER 5

My Mother's lips

Springvale

1957

Mother's hands are soft and silky. They can bake a chocolate and vanilla spiral cake; grow sweet-smelling tomatoes and beans that snap, and sew a warm, red wool coat with a matching red scarf.

Each day, I watched Mother put her soft hands to her lips picking at them until they cracked and bled. She does this automatically. Her fingers land on her lips as if drawn by a magnet. I watch her toying with her lips folding them back and forth on themselves as if they are alive and she is trying to stop words from spilling out of her mouth, holding them back barricading them with her fingers.

Mother always had a hand to her lips; except when she was cooking or cleaning. She picked at her lips until a tiny piece of skin is found and she lifts the skin edge slowly, deliberately and tears the skin across leaving a bright red gash that starts to bleed red.

It annoys me.

"Don't do that," I say to her one hundred times a day.

She stops momentarily.

She brushed her hands over her apron to stop them wandering but, within seconds her fingers slipped silently back to her lips and the picking and bleeding continues.

I think her lips must be dry from working in the garden under the hot sun. I buy her lip ointment with lanoline and smother her lips with these. They glisten momentarily. I carry a tube of ointment for her lips in my pocket. It has become a battle of wills. Whenever I see her picking her lips, I apply the creams. This happened many times a day. I wanted Mother to stop picking her lips. But she does not. Her lips crack and bleed and she cries out with the pain.

"See what you have done. I told you not to pick your lips," I said and slather more ointment on her lips.

Her lips bleed under the ointment.

I am the guardian of my mother's lips. But my determination to stop her picking at her lips never becomes a reality.

Mother talks to invisible voices. She has strange disturbing conversations with people I cannot see. They are real to her. Sometimes she speaks in loud, fluttering whispers to these voices. At other times, she rants and screams loudly at them, the noise fills our home. Sometimes, not often, the voices make her laugh and she giggles.

"What is the joke?" I asked.

Mother told me her friends are telling her funny stories. This makes me sad as she never laughs or tells jokes with me.

I hate it when the voices order her to strange things. They might refuse permission for Mother to sleep in her own bed. They tell her she must sleep in the bath. Sometimes I find her in the bath wrapped in a blanket.

The voices become louder at night, sometimes ordering her to walk around all night. She argues with the voices, she shouts and bangs doors.

"Stop it!" I yell.

I covered my head with my pillow.

Despite the closed bedroom door, I could still hear her creeping around, muttering to the voices. She opens my bedroom door, and I pretend to be asleep. She walks around my room whispering loudly, hisses at the voices.

Sometimes she pulls me out of bed and screams at me.

"You are in league with the Devil; the voices told me," she said, her face crumpled in fury.

"God knows I would never do that," I shout back.

She leaves the room, tears running down her face.

I drag myself out of bed and make us both a cup of tea.

She cries, and I sob.

I had no idea what to do.

~

One time, Mother made me go with her to the police station to report the voices for being nasty to her. I had to translate what she said to the police. They understood she was mentally ill and a doctor came in and took Mother away. She was admitted into a mental facility. When she came out, her skin had developed a yellow tinge and she was unsteady on her feet. Mother had a bad reaction to Largactil, the psychiatric medication she had been given.

She hated the medicine and stopped taking it.

"If you can make my mother better from her mental illness, I will be a missionary to the lepers in Africa for you," I said to God in my prayers.

But God did not hear me.

I never become a missionary.

~

Sometimes Mother changes back to my real mother. She hugs me and says she is proud of me. She cooks my favourite meal of roast chicken with crispy potatoes and stuffed tomatoes and beans made with her special tomato sauce. I am very happy in these moments.

Mother was a dressmaker and bought two metres of pink cotton material to make a dress for me. I watch her as she flips through the Vogue magazines she normally keeps on the top shelf in her bedroom cupboard. She takes out her retractable tape measure and draws out patterns on brown paper.

Mother always makes the hem longer and pins it up to allow me to grow into the dress. She cuts the pattern from stiff brown wrapping paper. She measures the brown paper against me to make sure it will fit. She takes the special gold scissors my father bought her from the sewing box.

I relish the sound of the gold scissors cutting through the brown paper pattern and the material pinned underneath. I love this part, watching her pin and cut, sometimes hitting a pin. Eventually, the pieces are pinned together, and she opens the wooden cabinet with the Singer sewing machine hidden inside. She lifts it from its special spot, oils the machine and sews. Father bought this machine for my mother when I was seven years old.

"Calel," she said to me. My name is Cally.

This is her pet name for me when she is well. Her soft hands stroke my face.

"Calel, you will look beautiful in this dress."

I smile and relax.

I pick up the leftover scraps of material to make small dresses for my doll Christine. She is a Mama doll and when you turn her over she says "Mama." Father bought me this doll.

Mother and I sew together. I love the sound of the intermittent whirl of the sewing machine. I have my tongue sticking out the side of my mouth as I attempt to thread a needle. I am sewing small pieces of fabric together, making Christine a dress too.

~

Mother started to pick her lips and talk to the voices after my father died. Mother loved us, I knew. But after Father died, her mental illness made her drift away from us. She became distant and different, developed a weird friendship with the voices and her invisible friends.

Mother was a beautiful woman with thick, black wavy hair and a gentle face that never seemed to wrinkle. But her lips were always cracked and bleeding.

Mother's continual picking at her lips became an indicator of her growing psychosis and she would become lost in her other world.

Seeing her pick at her lips created a sympathetic response in me and I developed dry lips. I sense dryness on my lips and apply ointment. I became obsessed with having the lip balm nearby and squeezed little amounts of the ointment into small glass pots in a variety of places such as my blue bag and in the drawer next to my bed. I saw the little pots as a type of insurance that would stop me picking my lips, afraid to be like her, guarding myself, watching for signs of the madness within me.

I never managed to stop Mother from picking at her lips. No one cured her schizophrenia, despite doctors prescribing medication that dulled the voices but had miserable side effects.

It took many years for me to understand her mental illness.

I still apply ointment on my lips whenever I feel dryness.

CHAPTER 6

The laundry

Springvale

1957

Our dog Taffy fancied himself as an acrobat. He used to eye newly washed sheets as they swung around on the Hills hoist, growling and cursing deep in his fur and, without warning, leap up on his small, fat legs and bite hard on the white sheets as they twirled around, excited and terrified. He was afraid to let go.

"You are a silly dog. You will hurt yourself one day," I said.

He made me laugh.

Mother said, "You are a bad dog."

She pulled him off the clothes and pushed him into his kennel.

His mad obsession with the sheets ended when Mother tied him next to his kennel on washing days. His displeasure reflected in his loud wailing and incessant barking as he stretched to the end of his chain. His running feet making an arc pounded into the grass.

In the corner of our backyard garden to the right of the back steps, grew a huge wall of thick, dizzy honeysuckle. Its intoxicating perfume filled the air and made life exuberant. The yellow flowers of the honeysuckle were hidden within the thick green foliage. The creeper created a small corner of the world, a canopy of secrets. Brown sparrows built small nests in the foliage. I would part the creepers and find tiny eggs nestled in small warm nests. Sometimes I pulled the flowers off the creeper and sucked their sweet stems. They tasted sugary like honey.

Our laundry, a small room, was the thoroughfare from the kitchen to the backyard. The kitchen opened to the laundry on one side. There was another door from the laundry to the toilet and a third door to the outside yard. The side wall of the laundry had hooks for raincoats and jackets; underneath them were wooden slats for boots and shoes.

The laundry had two hard cement tubs situated at waist level near the copper against the wall, a tap over each trough. The round shiny copper had a heavy metal green lid. When I lowered the lid, it clanged like a chime. Inside the copper lived the Rinso washing powder, cleaning rags, a small cricket bat, and scrubbing brush. A small metal watertap over the top of the copper.

The walls of the laundry were painted a crisp white, a snowy curtain fluttered in the open window. On the floor, green and white linoleum set out in small squares, the same as the kitchen and bathroom.

My job on Saturdays was to wait until Mother waxed the floor and then slip and slide over the waxed linoleum to make the floor shine. I used a pair of old green Army socks over my feet and pretended I was a famous ice skater and would pivot and turn and bow to my imaginary audience.

Mondays were wash days. It always started with Mother counting out the shillings in the glass jar under the kitchen sink for the gas meter. She would place the shillings in her brown and -white checked apron pocket. She always wore this apron on wash days. Mother kneeled to feed the coins into the gas meter, which was hidden near the copper. The shillings dropped with a clank (if empty) or a thick thud (if full). The sound of the meter depended on the meter man's visit and the emptying of the meter.

Mother would light the gas jet with the matches in the pocket of her apron. The metallic smell of the gas and the roar of gas jets as they glowed blue, signalled the start of wash day.

"Have you a shilling?"

Mother asked if she did not have enough shillings for the wash.

I would search my Sunday school purse until I found a shilling.

On washing days, the copper was emptied of its contents and filled halfway with cold water. Rinso was carefully measured from a small, white cracked cup. As the water boiled in the copper, the house filled with the clean smell of Rinso washing powder.

Dirty sheets had already been collected from beds, as were the clothes from the clothes basket.

"Can you please collect the tea towels off their drying hooks?" Mother said.

I would run to collect the tea towels, remember the bath towels, and check the bedrooms for any soiled clothes.

Mother separated the whites, colours, and delicate clothes into small piles to be washed separately. Heavily soiled clothes such as my brothers' football socks and shorts were placed in a metal bucket with a measured amount of White King bleach to soak.

When the water in the copper water started to bubble and become hot and steamy, the whites would be put into the boiling water and pushed down and turned over with the old, cracked cricket bat belonging to one of my brothers. The bat had whitened over time; the handle remained a strange, darker colour.

The laundry became hazy with the soap and steam.

Sometimes the copper would overflow with water and soap if too many clothes were put in at once. Soap would dribble down the side of the copper and extinguish the gas jet, and a pungent smell of gas would leak into the air.

Mother would shout, "Oh, no."

She would empty the overflow boiling water into the sink, mop the floor, and relight the gas jet.

The clothes in the bubbling copper were periodically turned and rotated as they softened by the boiling water. Later, the clothes would be dragged out of the hot soapy stew with the stick. Mother methodically scrubbed the clothes by hand with a smaller wooden scrubbing brush. White shirt collars and cuffs would get special attention. In those days, a good housekeeper was judged by the whiteness of these collars and cuffs. Mother would scrub the clothes, then rinse them in another tub which had Blueo added to the water to make the whites even whiter.

I would hold onto my doll Christine. She was naked on wash days, her clothes already placed in the delicate pile.

Mother would perspire heavily, sweat rolling down her face and into the crevices of her dress. Every so often, she would stop and mutter, "God, help me" under her breath and wipe her brow with her apron, bend backwards holding her back, and sigh. She would wipe her hands on her apron and sit at the kitchen table for a few minutes picking at her lips and muttering words I never understood.

When Mother returned to the laundry, the wet clothes would be squeezed and twisted by hand. Great rivers of water cascaded down into the sink, soaking Mother and her apron. The wringing had been the hardest part. Mother was only a small woman; the large, wet sheets were almost too much for her to pull out of the water and twist and turn.

"Can you hold this?" she asked me.

I held the end of a wet sheet as Mother twisted the wet material until gushes of water came out. Then a thick thud as the wrung sheet was tossed into the clothes basket.

She lifted her hands to her head, wiping her face with the now soaked apron.

The familiar symphony of sound, water running, sloshing of wrung clothes, whirling of the gas jets, Mother groaning and muttering, her hair wet. The front of her dress and apron saturated.

"Calel," she called. "Calel; can you help me lift the basket please?"

I carefully held one end of the cane basket with two hands, both of us and the basket dripping with water would go down the steps, past the honeysuckle and its sweet perfume to the backyard.

The twisted wet clothes were shaken out firmly, smoothed carefully onto the Hills Hoist wires. Mother would grab hold of the wire with one hand, hanging on to it to stop it spinning around. Then she would pick six wooden pegs at a time from the metal tin attached to the Hills Hoist and place the pegs in her apron pocket.

She would lift an article of clothes out of the clothes basket and peg it carefully with the wooden pegs. There had been an order to the way the clothes were hung on the line. The underwear and cleaning rags were hidden in the innermost rails of the Hills Hoist. Then trousers, shirts, skirts, and school uniforms next. Jumpers placed on cords were stretched out to prevent peg marks. On the outside wires were sheets and towels. Mother would bend, grab the pegs, grab the wire, and peg the clothes. Basket after basket after basket carried out until done.

Mother would go back to the laundry and scrub the coloured clothes, delicate clothing, and cleaning cloths. After four trips to the Hills Hoist, she would wind it up and it would spin a riot of white and colour.

Christine and I noted where her pink dress and white jacket and underpants were placed on the line.

Our dog Taffy would go mad, barking, pulling at his chain jumping up in the air, rushing about.

"Shh," Mother said.

Back in the laundry, the copper had to be emptied; clear water poured onto the vegetable plants in the garden. The floor mopped. The end of washing day would be signalled by the mop being placed upside down against the outside wall.

Mother flushed, wet and breathless would fill the aluminium whistling kettle with water and feed another shilling into the gas meter.

"Calel, you have been a great help; come and have a cup of tea with me," she said.

We shared a cup of hot Bushel's tea poured into the shining orange cups. Ate a sweet almond biscuit from the round tin, which lived on the second shelf.

Mother would be quiet, sip her tea, and look out the window at the wash spinning around. The dog now hysterical, barking and straining at the chain; he was tantalised to madness.

When she could not bear his noise anymore, Mother would find a bone and take it out to him.

"Shush," she said.

Taffy would munch on his bone with one beady eye on the washing line, giving a deep growl every so often.

CHAPTER 7

Graphology

Springvale

1957

The sun stopped shining for me after my beloved Father's death. Mother cried all day, every day. My brothers were strangely quiet. Our family lived in daily sadness, depression, deprivation. I was numb and unable to fully understand what was happening. I had recurring dreams where Father came home and told me he was alive. He said that another man had been killed; it was the man to whom he had lent his coat to use. I woke up wanting to believe the dream.

As a naive ten-year-old girl, I often searched the night sky, wondered which star my Father had become. Mother had told he was in heaven and now a shining star. But to me, the stars seemed too far away.

Even as I write this to recall memories from that time, it fills me with unprotected feelings.

Mother used to say I had been Father's favourite and attached to that medal of honour stood extreme emptiness and pain at his death.

I was a serious child. I developed an interest in graphology. Not sure how or why I became interested in graphology. But I was an enthusiastic early reader who read everything in print, books, magazines, even bits of paper. My habit was to sneak in corners reading when I should have been doing my chores at home. Each year, I would read the contents of the class library cupboard, hating the fact that I could only take out two books a week from the library.

Friend Rosy and I would pretend we were part of a group called The Secret Seven. Enid Blyton wrote several stories about The Secret Seven. We devoured those stories. The two of us would search for potentially dangerous people in the street and make up crime stories about them.

"I think he looks suspicious," said Rosy.

She pointed to a large tattooed man working on the roads. "He looks like a criminal."

We hovered near him taking notes about his appearance.

"Do you think we should report him to the police?" she said.

"No, he hasn't done anything bad yet," I said.

Perhaps I read an article in a *Women's Weekly* magazine about graphology and learnt that it was the study and analysis of handwriting. I remember being excited by this promise of having secret powers that enabled me to read into people's minds through their handwriting. I borrowed many books on graphology from the council libraries. Then I made copious notes about types of keystrokes and their meanings. In those days, I had a blue exercise book for my graphology notes. It was deemed special by me and covered with brown paper and plastic cover for protection. The notebook had an air of importance and I carried it with me everywhere.

At times, I entertained myself by analysing friends' scribbles and teachers' blackboard writing looking for clues as to who they really were.

My English pen-friend Chris had small, tiny, tight writing. This intrigued me. Her letters would come in blue aerogramme paper and the words looked as though a machine had typed them. I loved receiving her letters. We wrote to each other about mundane things related to school and friends.

Chris and I had been pen-friends for forty years when we finally met in person many years later in London. To my delight, Chris was as organised and precise in all matters of her life as her writing had revealed this to me years ago.

As a student in class, I enjoyed observing our teachers' blackboard writing to learn if the teachers were secretly cruel or stingy or untrustworthy. I would smile if Miss Johnstone wrote on the board with long elaborate loops of y and g, for I knew she had a love of luxury and expensive tastes. Would envisage her home with gold taps in the bathrooms and marble benches, heavy red velvet drapes at her windows as had seen in *Women's Weekly* homes of movie stars.

John and Jim teased me about my interest in graphology.

"You are one weird little sister," said Jim.

"Calel, put your exercise book down and help me with the dishes," Mother said.

However, friends were curious. "Would you analyse my writing?"

I would make careful notes about the sample of handwriting the friend gave me, being mindful not to say if I discovered evidence of cruelty, such as the writer had pressed too hard on the page, instead saying that the person had passion.

"Graphology is a science. You can detect forgeries and contest signatures and wills," I said.

Today, I understand people who do this are not graphologists but called forensic document examiners.

I read that graphology had a role in medicine and could assist in the diagnosis of someone with mental illness or Parkinson's disease. The muscular movements involved in writing were controlled by the central nervous system and these movements correspond with the muscular tension of our hands. These were mostly unconscious. I copied these words carefully into my exercise book and even though I did not fully understand the meaning; it all sounded grand and scientific.

"Mother, can you write a sentence for me?" I asked.

But I was never sure if her shaky writing was due to illness or her lack of confidence in English.

Some people suggest graphology can predict the future like astrology, but in my opinion, this is untrue as handwriting can reveal only your current mood.

Generally, I was a timid, quiet child who hung back and preferred to be in the background. Photos of me at that time showed a serious young girl, short in stature, with brown plaits with sausage curls at the end.

The class teacher heard of my hobby.

"Would you like to give a small talk to the class about your hobby?" she asked.

Normally I would have run a mile rather than stand in front of our class and talk, but this was different. I felt very excited about graphology.

I crept to the front of the class. I felt exposed as everyone waited for me to speak. The class sat cramped on the floor in the green room. The walls were covered with lions and giraffes from Africa. The bottom row of classroom windows was pushed out to open and let in the fresh air. Light filtered in from the sloping glass in the ceiling. We had wooden desks with inkwells. The desks creaked and scraped, the desktops banged nosily as students closed them.

"I have been asked our teacher to speak about

my hobby of graphology....” I broke off as my voice disappeared.

The teacher smiled and nodded me to continue.

“I will teach you how to learn about yourself,” I said. My words came out in a rush.

I stood on tiptoes at the blackboard, clutching with sweaty fingers the new piece of white chalk that the teacher handed me. My voice, soft at first, grew in volume as I became confident.

Carefully and cautiously, I drew several lines on the blackboard in white chalk indicating upper, lower, and middle zones of writing. Using a yellow piece of chalk, I wrote letters for the upper zones such as ‘t’ and ‘h.’ Then the middle range such as ‘a,’ ‘c,’ ‘m,’ and ‘n’ and the lower zones to show ‘g,’ ‘y,’ and ‘p.’

“Extroverted people slope their writing forward; introverted slope their writing backwards,” I said, giving examples.

“Happy writing rides up; sad down.”

The class reviewed their own writing.

“Can you tell if a person is a murderer by their writing?” one child asked.

“Can you tell if a person is lying?” another student asked.

I tried to answer as best I could. I used examples showing heavy, thick writing and coloured chalk for emphasis.

At the end of my short talk, the class burst into spontaneous applause. I smiled a wide smile.

Whilst I analysed other's writing, it took a great deal of effort to make sure my own writing had all the hallmarks of a well-balanced person. I made sure that I had the right loops and lower flourishes and developed careful elegant writing.

One year, my classmates and teacher voted my writing the best in class. And I became the official 'Queen of Handwriting.' The teacher handed me a blue and gold embossed certificate with my name and new status. She wrote my name on the role of honour on the wall, next to the 'Queen and King of arithmetic and spelling.'

Feeling confident, I entered a state writing competition in a newspaper for beautiful writing and won a Schaeffer fountain pen. The pen was a good weight and cool to touch, navy blue with a gold top that screwed on tightly.

At that time, we had a blue budgerigar named Dennis who was very tame and would run down my arm and peck at his reflection in the gold top when I wrote at my desk at home.

He would peck at the top and chirp, "Dennis is a pretty boy."

This made me laugh.

When the fountain pen ink ran out, I would carefully unscrew the fountain pen and place the ink chamber with the nib in the dark blue inkwell and pressed on its ink bladder. The ink made a swoosh sound as it sucked up. I often had blue, inky fingers that left blue marks on everything I touched. But I cherished my fountain pen and believed it a lucky talisman for me.

One day, the zippered pen bag with my fountain pen and pencils disappeared. I spent tearful weeks searching for the pen, daily attending the lost property office at school.

"Has anyone handed in a zippered blue bag containing pen and pencils?" I asked every few days.

But it was never found.

Today, I still possess the exercise book with my graphology notes. My writing is now extremely untidy and messy. Nevertheless, I remember my hobby with great affection as it assisted me through a river of uncertainty after my father's death.

I still peek at individual's writing and guess at their personality.

CHAPTER 8

Our home

Springvale

1958

There are eight rooms in our home. Mother's room is in the front of the house; it gets very hot in summer and is freezing in winter. My bedroom is at the back and faces the backyard.

The house is Mother's domain although I am allowed some leeway with my room. We have white Venetian blinds on the window in every bedroom. Cleaning the Venetians is my most hated job. Each Saturday, I clean each slate with a warm, soapy cloth to remove the dust and grime and then wipe and dry. It takes forever.

Mother made flowered curtains and a matching cover for the armchair in the corner of my room. The armchair belonged to one of her friends. Mother made the cotton cover as a surprise one day and now the room feels fresh and new. There is a small cushion for my back.

Mostly I keep the curtains open, especially when there is a full moon. Love to watch the moon's rays fill the room. A row of red roses has been planted outside my bedroom. When the wind blows, the rose bushes scratch the window and wake me up. It sounds like someone is tapping on my window.

My room is the best. It collects the morning sun and is airy. John and Jim's room is between Mother's and mine. My walls are painted a light lilac. Mother and I painted both our rooms one school holidays.

There is a desk against the window; it has a tablecloth and a sheet of clear plastic to protect it. The wooden desk belonged to Jim, but he doesn't use it anymore. The shelves on one side of the desk have my school books and a Bible. There is a drawer in the desk where I hide my diary.

I sometimes sit at the desk pretending to do homework, eating bacon crisp biscuits. A novel secreted under my school homework book. Or I read under the covers by torchlight. I borrow two books from the class library and read them in quick succession. We only have a few books and wish we could afford more.

"What would you like for your birthday?" Mother asked.

"Can I choose a book?" I said.

Rosy lent me *The Diary of Ann Frank* and *The Footsteps of Ann Frank*. After reading the books, I decided to write a diary and call my diary Wendy. Every day I would write to Wendy; she became my one true friend.

A small bookshelf to the side of the room holds an old set of encyclopaedia and other books belonging to the family. The shelf is homemade but sturdy. A couple of John's suitcases sit in the corner. On the other side of the door is the green shopping jeep. There is nowhere else to put it.

The wooden cupboard holds my clothes. It has six drawers and on top a small cupboard. My best dress, the white woollen one with a white jacket, is kept in Mother's cupboard.

The bedroom door opens to the hall and bathroom.

Usually, I have everything ready the night before school; I place the clothes for tomorrow on the chair.

The mattress is old and lumpy. Mother placed a cross with Jesus above my bed for protection.

~

If Mother has been listening to the voices during the day, I escaped to my room when I came home from school. I know the signs. Once I read a psychology book about paranoid schizophrenia. I know the description fits Mother perfectly.

Who do I turn to? There is no one to help me.

Once, in desperation, I penned a letter to *The Sun* psychologist who wrote back personally to tell me to make sure to take Mother to see a doctor. I took her to the doctor, but the doctor did nothing as I had to translate everything for the doctor and Mother admitted nothing.

John is currently working as a jackaroo on a

property near Mildura. He sends money home to Mother each payday. Jim is around but involved in his own life as has fallen in love with a girl called Jill. Her father runs a funeral parlour. Jim brought home a wide purple ribbon from the funeral parlour.

Mother's illness caused problems with Jim and Jill's relationship.

The lounge room has a small fireplace, which is not used now. Instead, we have an electric bar heater in the fireplace that has imitation burning logs when hot.

"I have a surprise for you both," Jim said one day.

He carried a small, second-hand black-and-white TV and placed it on the table. It had two metal antennae which Jim had to be fiddle with or the screen would go black. The three of us watched every program that first night, even the epilogue.

In the evenings, Mother and Jim watch TV in the lounge room. I am only allowed to join them after I have completed my homework. A silly program we all like is Graeme Kennedy's show, "In Melbourne Tonight" with the barrel girl called Panda.

Jim is always there for us. He buys furniture through the shop where he works. People bring in old furniture for a trade-in on a new piece. Often these are discarded to the tip, but Jim bought a few that were traded in good condition. Jim does the male stuff, painting the outside of the house, sometimes mowing the lawns.

Jim has always been Mother's favourite; she never sees my side of any argument. Jim is good to Mother but bossy with me.

At one stage, Jim bought an old bomb of a car and spent enormous amounts of time trying to fix it, going to wreckers for bits, borrowing car manuals from the library.

"And here is something for you Mother, so you don't have sore hands," he said one day.

He dragged in a second-hand washing machine. Mother had an infection in her hands from scrubbing clothes by hand. The washing machine worked perfectly.

Mother is reliant on the money Jim brings home to pay bills. Money is always scarce.

The back door opens to the garden. Along the top of the fence near the gate is a wooden box for the milkman. If I am awake when he passes about 1 a.m., I can hear the soft clip-clop of the milkman's horse. The milkman tells him 'stop' or 'start.' Then the clatter of milk bottles as they go into our box. Sometimes the milkman swears if he drops a bottle of milk. The exact money is needed and a note as to how many milk bottles. A simple system and it works.

Most Sundays, on our return from church, Mother and I garden. I trim the edges of the lawn with hand-clippers while leaning on my knees. I remove the weeds that grow on the fence from the outside. My hands become stained with grass. After a while, my hands ache from using the clippers and my knees hurt. I stand up and stretch and watch people go by.

A large, wooden broom is used to push the cuttings and weeds together. Mother digs around the roses. We have red roses along one side in the front, white lilies and red carnations in another part. There is a flowering pink blossom tree near the front door. Mother bought the tree when I was sick in bed with the measles. She carried it all the way from the shops; a long way. She planted it carefully near the front porch. Each year the tree is covered in pink blossoms. Blue and pink Hydrangeas bloom under the lounge room window.

We have a push lawn mower which Mother uses. Jim used to do the mowing; now he is out with his girlfriend.

The backyard has apple and apricot trees. There is an old wooden tool shed and an older outdoor toilet. I hated going to the outdoor toilet as a child as it had spiders that dangled from the roof and made me squeal. My brothers used to torment me by banging on the outside wall when I was on the toilet. I used to sprint to and from the toilet at night, always fearful. Now we have sewerage connected and a nice indoor flush toilet.

The extensive vegetable garden has neat rows of broad beans, beans, carrots, silver beet, lettuce, potatoes, and tomatoes. Mother looks after these as well; we always have masses of vegetables. It is my job to bring in the vegetables for the meal. I love the broad beans and eat them off the plants. We rely on the vegetable garden for our food; we share extra garden produce with the neighbours. The potatoes are a delight to harvest; big, round and plump, hiding underground, attached to a tuber. I enjoy digging to the length and width of the potato plant, sometimes striking a potato with a crunch when the fork catches caught on a large one. The small green ones are left in the ground. My Mother knows a lot about gardening; everything she plants grows.

"Don't ever eat the green ones as they will make you sick," Mother said.

"And don't dig all the potatoes up at once, you need to leave some for nutrients in the soil."

My pile of potatoes is buried treasure to me. Meals made with these big bumpy spuds swallow up delicious herbs and spices in stews. My favourite food is crunchy roast potatoes, chips, and tasty potato cakes.

I hold a romantic notion of comfort food which includes chips and potato cakes.

We keep six brown and white chickens in a chicken shed in the far corner of the house.

Taffy's kennel is near the old toilet.

My dog and I often sit on the back step. He used to belong to a school friend. Her father planned to put the dog down as he kept digging up the garden beds. My friend begged me to have him. He is mine now and loves to run along the fence and bark at people as they pass. He enjoys his walks with me but becomes so excited he needs to pee every five minutes.

The back neighbours can see us from their kitchen.

Mother mutters about them, "They are spying on me."

I know this is not true.

There are other neighbours she feels are against her. She talks loudly in Greek about them. It freaks me out as they seem nice to me.

Mother's few friends are from the church, the Woman's Guild at the Church of England. Mrs Allen has an unusual home with drawers overflowing with shiny and velvet material, all types of lace and cottons. Her house is like a shop. She is always making dolls and clothes for fetes or gifts.

Mrs Allen has six brown hens.

"They are my girls," Mrs Allen said.

As soon as she clucks for them, they come running. The hens roam free in her garden and are tame. Mr Allen is a Justice of the Peace and signs any legal documents for us.

They have no children.

The Church of England is far away from our home. It takes about fifty minutes to walk to the church. Sometimes a neighbour picks us up in her car. One day this lady jammed her finger in the car door as she closed it. We all tried to help. Mother worried about this lady as she lived alone. She asked me to take her special Greek cakes to cheer her up, which it did.

On certain rostered Saturdays, Mother does the flowers for the church. I accompany her, use the time to check out the church, and sort the hymn books. Each Sunday, I attend Sunday school and have made my Confirmation. My Sunday school teacher is nice; we create stories about Jesus on felt boards.

~

Once I attended a church camp at Arthur's Seat. This was a major adventure for me. We travelled to camp in the back of a removal truck, singing songs at the top of our voices all the way. No one wore seat belts. Not sure how Mother afforded it. I remember having a five-pound note with me, which I handed in. Perhaps we gave a nominal amount. Each child had a room at the camp and we were ordered to keep it tidy. Each day, the leaders undertook room inspection. I won a certificate for the neatest room. We hiked, had singing contests, and prayed and enjoyed hot chocolate drinks at night.

Mother and her friend Mrs Hicks came to the camp on Parents Day. But I did not spend much time with Mother and Mrs Hicks, as I was eager to return to the exciting games the leaders had organised for us.

When I returned from the camp, I remember

Mother looking as cold as ice as she reached for the dreaded black strap.

“You ignored Mrs Hicks and me. This was very rude. We drove a long way to be with you. And you ran off. I was so ashamed.”

“You are an ungrateful girl,” she said, face red with fury.

The memory of the sudden beating stayed with me and how unfair it was.

And I held deep guilt for making Mother sad and ignoring her.

CHAPTER 9

Whiteside State School

Springvale

1957

I love school. Enjoy the classes and the games. But hate folk dancing because I must dance with boys with warts on their hands. I never excelled at sport but play rounders and gave it my best shot. I am such a bookworm and was delighted when I was nominated library monitor. Normally I am a good student and do well in class and exams, and my writing is always neat.

At one stage, I remember sitting in the front row and blinking at the blackboard, trying to make sense of the faded words the teacher had written in chalk on the board. Soon after the doctors came to the school and every child was measured for height, weight, and vision. The doctor said I had become short-sighted and needed glasses.

"The three bouts of measles affected your eyes," said the doctor.

Mother and I caught the train to the Eye and Ear Hospital to obtain a pair of glasses for me. I was ecstatic when the glasses were ready. They were pale pink plastic and a little old-fashioned. Everything was fresh and bright for the first time in my life. I could see small details such as the blades of grass and leaves on trees.

"I will be able to see the teacher's chalk work perfectly now," I said.

Mother nodded her head. "You can be top of your class if work very hard at your lessons."

"Hello, four eyes," said Jim when he came home.

I don't care. I can see.

Each morning at primary school, the whole school lines up in rows to drink the compulsory milk. The students march in pairs to the milk crates. Each student takes a small bottle of milk from the green crates which are packed with milk bottles. We gulp the milk under teacher supervision. Some children don't like the milk because it heats up quickly on hot days and tastes funny. One time the teachers handed out chocolate-flavoured straws which improved the taste of the milk.

Mother lets me put Ovaltine flavouring in my milk at home. It tastes like a chocolate milkshake.

My school had a long corridor from one end to the other to the building to the toilets. Once I had to deliver a message to another class and marvelled at how many classrooms there were in the school. The classes were mostly quiet; teachers were strict in those days.

Being ink monitor was fun. I filled the ink pots but had diluted the dark ink to a lighter shade of blue that I preferred. We write with wooden pens which have steel nibs, dipped in ink. A blotter is required to mop up the extra ink so it does not smudge.

I lived in an alternative universe at school, felt comfortable and happy, had friends.

At home, everything was different.

Mother earned money by working long hours making dresses for the locals. She was an expert dressmaker. I remember a neighbour's daughter came for a fitting for a ball gown. It was green taffeta with tiny pleats at the sleeves bodice. It was the most beautiful dress I had ever seen. I could picture her dancing and being the belle of the ball, like Cinderella. Mother stayed up all night finishing the dress. She sewed and muttered to herself. Somehow despite the mental illness, Mother found the power and strength to sew, cook, clean, garden, and keep the family together.

It must have been a very difficult and lonely life for her.

CHAPTER 10

My friend Rosy

Springvale

1958

When I return home from school, Taffy rushes out to greet me. His doggie face lights up in a smile.

"Good boy," I said and pat and stroke him.

"Do you want to play?" I said.

He grabs an old tennis ball in his mouth. Spittle runs down his mouth and he drops the ball at my feet.

"Fetch." I throw the ball.

He dashes after it, bringing it back triumphant.

Then I chase him around the yard until we are both puffing.

We are companions on the back step, the dog and I, and I ruffle his fur as he likes it.

"I learnt a new way to skip today—French skipping with two ropes. You have to skip zigzag not to get caught in the twirling ropes," I tell the dog.

He gives me a lick of encouragement and I hug him. My dog knows all my secrets; things that I cannot tell anyone else.

The honeysuckle perfume is strong and sweet in the background.

Eventfully, I open the screen door, search for Mother. I am always on edge, watch for cues, and stare at her face. If she smiles and is happy to see me, everything is fine. She hugs me, and we share a cup of tea and small Greek delicacy that she has cooked.

"How was your day, Calel?" she said in Greek. "How did you do in the spelling test?"

The night before Mother helped me with my spelling. She read the words with difficulty, as her English is limited. I wrote the words and we checked them together.

"You are getting better," she said, giving me a hug.

Last month, Mother commenced English by Correspondence Course so she could help me with my school work. The lessons are in pictures and written in Greek and English. She works hard on the words, sitting at the kitchen table with pencil and rubber.

"We are both school girls," she said and laughed.

But when I come home, and she is distant, her eyes glazed, muttering to herself. I cringe. She is likely to get the black strap from the kitchen and hit me, scream abuse about things I know nothing about.

"Stop," I shout.

"It is me, Cally."

She stops, covers her face with her hands, puts her head on the table and sobs.

Did the voices tell her?

Did I do something wrong?

"It is all right," I said. "It didn't hurt." I lie.

She holds my hands, tears stream down her crumpled face, black hair in disarray and holds me to her.

"I am so sorry. I am so sorry."

With a heavy heart, I start on my chores. Feed the chooks, collect the eggs. Go to the shops. Sneak reading if I can get away with it.

~

Rosy lives at number nine Ericksen Street and I live in number eleven. But there is a corner house between us. So, she lives a few doors down. Rosy is one month and three days older than me. She is artistic, has long, red hair done in a horsey tail. She is tall, and I am short. I have known Rosy since I was eight and we have been good friends for years.

My friend Rosy and I walk to school together. We attend Whiteside State School, not far from where we live.

"Why do you have to do so many chores after school?" Rosy asked.

Rosy cannot understand that I must translate and write letters for Mother.

"You are a child and should be allowed to be a child," Rosy said.

In her eyes, I am exploited. Her life is carefree. I never saw it like that. I knew I had to help Mother with written work; it was my responsibility.

I am older than my years having to be the translator, the writer of letters, and the bridge for my Mother.

She, in turn, makes beautiful meals. Sews lovely clothes, does what she can. I practice being grateful for everything.

"Hurry up with your jobs and let's play murders," Rosy said. She loves this game. Brother Jim thinks the game is stupid.

"Can I play murders too?" he asked, making mock of us.

Sometimes we play at Rosy's house. We swing on her swing and read her mother's books. Rosy's Mother is elegant, always wears red lipstick and black high heels and rose-pattered waisted dresses and stockings. She has dark red hair with a deep wave in the front. My mother sews dresses for Rosy's Mother and sews girly dresses with wide collars that are fashionable for Rosy. Mother takes extra time with Rosy's sewing as she has a curved spine and it is difficult to get suitable clothes. Rosy drives my mother to distraction as she hates being fitted for clothes, yells if a pin touches her.

Rosy's Mother and Father are kind to me.

Rosy has elaborate birthday parties, types of games I am unfamiliar with: pass the parcel, pin the tail on the donkey, musical chairs. The party table loaded with sausage rolls, cakes, and plates of hundreds and thousands of sandwiches. There are other children at these parties, but I do not know them. They are not from our neighbourhood.

We never have birthday parties at my house since Father died.

Rosy receives pocket money, a strange concept for me. She buys sweets and places portions in matchboxes, rations them out over the week. She is disciplined.

Rosy is an only child with concerned parents. I enjoy the wilder part of Rosy but could never be as strong as she is; it was never an option for me.

I am a quiet friend, play Rosy's games, aware I am a guest. Know my place.

I fed Rosy's cat while they were on holiday. Rosy's Mother gave me a collection of little cans of Spam for the cat. I swung on her swing and wondered what it would be like to live in her family.

Once, a little girl that Mother looked after came with me to feed the cat. She ran into the swing while I was swinging and hurt her head slightly. I felt guilty and sad. Mother berated me for my selfishness when I should have been looking after the girl.

I never tell Rosy about home and problems with Mother. She lives in another secure world; she would never understand.

We talk of school and friends.

CHAPTER 11

Home life

Springvale

1959

I have learnt not to make waves at home. There are enough there already. Mother now shouts profanities at anyone who whistles near her.

"Stop whistling at me, I know you are in league with the devil," she shouts in Greek.

"You are deliberately tormenting me."

People turn and stare at this short dark-haired woman and shrug their shoulders and keep whistling. It has become part of her illness and it scares me witless; I never feel safe. I am always praying to God to help me. Am always holding my breath, waiting for the next mad episode.

At some level, my child's brain knows that I am loved and cared for, but terrified at this growing weird behaviour by my Mother.

Once Mother forced me to go to the neighbour's house to tell him to stop whistling at her. Mother was adamant that it is a secret sign to make her suffer. She watched me from our house as I knocked on the neighbour's door, made small talk to the neighbour about life and school, and left and never mentioned the whistling.

He must have thought me a strange girl.

I informed Mother he whistled because he was happy and would try to stop whistling.

She shook her head.

Mother is capable of much warmth and kindness; is the first to help anyone sick or ailing. But she has this other dark, dangerous part that lashes out and consumes me. I try to be the best little girl in the world so as not to upset her. But of course, I can never be.

My biggest fear is I will develop the same mental illness as Mother. Try to keep a good hold of myself. Watch for signs that I am going mad; check myself to see if I am unreasonable or crazy. And I never discovered normal.

CHAPTER 12

Secondary school

Springvale

1960 and beyond

Mother looks after two small, Greek toddlers while their parents work in a local factory. They drop the children off at our home early on their way to work and pick them up after their shifts had finished. Mother loves the children and is kind and generous with them. The parents of the children are very happy with the care the children receive from Mother. She makes nourishing meals for them, puts them down for a sleep in the afternoon and plays games and reads to them. This keeps her busy while I was at school.

My secondary education commenced at Springvale High School in 1960 and I became a small fish in a big school of 1,000 students. The route from home to Springvale High stretches to a quarter of a mile and takes me more than thirty minutes to walk from home to school. Usually, I sprint past the wooded area on the outside of the football ground as it is scary. There are rumours of people being hurt there. Few people take the shortcut through the football ground as strange men loiter there. When I reach the Ericksen factory, I slow down to a walk as it is populated with workers coming and going.

I remember being caught in a massive storm on my way home and saturated to the bone.

"Go and change out of your wet things, then eat. I cooked you a plate of hot chips to warm you up," Mother said.

It was just what I needed.

I am lost at the high school; there were so many students there and many buildings dotted around the school. Running from one class to the other, I sometimes become confused. High school opened a new era for me. In the first form, I was placed in an all-girls form. The girls are nice. We were all newbies and anxious and needed each other.

Rosy walks home with me sometimes, but she is in a different form at school. We both became friends with a red-haired girl named Lyn, who was an excellent swimmer. Her Mother coaches swimming.

"Go Lyn, go," shouts the school as one at swimming sports.

The pressure is on for Lyn to win every swimming race. She has become the school's dedicated legend and tops the class in most subjects.

The following year in form two, I am placed in a mixed form of boys and girls. It is a great year for me; I love my classes, enjoy the teachers, and have many friends.

Some teachers stand out for the wrong reasons. Mr Sirrell takes us for French. He is fond of making long speeches on the usefulness of French. He is cruel and enjoys making fun of students, putting them down.

"What do you want? How dare you disturb my class?" he said to any hapless student sent to his class to deliver a message from the Headmaster.

He dislikes distractions to his kingdom.

"You," he said signalling some poor female student.

"Stop staring at John and get your brain back to the French lesson. I know you have a crush on him."

Both John and the female student are mortified and then teased by others.

His idea of power is to humiliate vulnerable students. He never picked on those who fought back and traded insults. He "married me up" with one boy and I hated it, blushing red with emotion. Mr Sirrell thought it funny.

"Look at Cally blushing," he said, and everyone turned to look at me.

I put the textbook over my face and tried to hide, wanting to disappear. At recess, others would continue with the teasing. I can never forget the torment, especially as Mr Sirrell carried the theme of me and this other boy for the whole year in class.

I had been a quiet industrious student but hated French because of him.

I remember when the school inspectors came

to check on the teachers. They sat at the back of the class and watched the class and interaction. Mr Sirrell did a dummy run with the class before they came; therefore, we knew the answers and regularly put our hands up. It was staged, and I wondered if the inspectors guessed.

Mr Carruthers for science is an excellent teacher. He is Scottish and has a broad accent. I embrace science because of him, read and learn as much as I could in science. The experiments were the best part, mixing chemicals for a reaction, making rotten egg gas.

We learn in science that another spaceman has orbited the earth. It is becoming a race between America and Russia to see who will be the first to reach the moon. The first into space was Major Yuri Gagarin. His whole orbit lasted 108 minutes and the orbit had a maximum height of 187 miles. His spaceship weighed five tons and was named *Vostok 1*.

I could not grasp that a man could orbit the earth.

Alan Shepard became the first American astronaut to go into space and return. Since then, rocket after rocket, spaceman after spaceman, have been sent up. Maybe one day we will land on the moon. I expect one day we will take a rocket and fly to the moon to see our friends there.

America always tells the world about their successes and failures. Not so with Russia; only their successes. We don't know how many have failed. No one hears much beyond the Iron Curtain which is Russia. Tourists are forbidden unless they have special permits. There is always anxiety that America and Russia will go to war and explode deadly bombs that will kill us all. America is also making deadly bombs. I read a book where the author stated that one lot of planet debris was perhaps a planet destroyed by a bomb. The planetoids could be the remains of a planet. Maybe they had a war and blew the world to smithereens. We talk about it at school. No one feels safe.

One teacher took us for arithmetic; he always looks sad and cannot control the class. The boys sense his weakness and became deliberately unruly. Years later I heard he had a nervous breakdown and had been admitted into a mental hospital.

Sport is not my thing; I am not good at it. I rarely manage to connect the bat with the ball in rounders. I never win a race, more likely to be near last. Rosy and I make daisy chains between breaks in sport. She is like me, can see no sense in sport. However, at one stage I did play volleyball and managed to stay on a team that played against other schools but was too short to be a star.

~

In 1962, fires swept through the Dandenongs, the foothills and mountains beyond. At least twenty-seven homes were destroyed, and eight people died.

The sky became a dirty black and red with smoke, dark like a partial solar eclipse. We could smell the burning trees from our classrooms.

CHAPTER 13

A typical day

Springvale

1961

Normally I wake at 6:45 a.m. open my eyes and notice how warm my bed is, dreading the thought of jumping into a freezing room. Finally, I push the blankets back and creep out. The house is icy. Mother is up preparing breakfast. Half asleep, I wash and climb into my school uniform. If Jim beats me to the bathroom, I make my bed and collect the newspaper.

My job is to let the chickens out of the henhouse.

"Morning," I said to the chuckling hens.

They push and shove like children behind the door as I open the hen house door, "Out you go." They scamper out excited by the new day, circle around me, squawking. I mix a thick goo of pollard and kitchen scraps and water. They cluck their approval and scoff their breakfast.

My weekend job is to clean the chicken pen. It is not a job I enjoy, I but have a system. Using a thick broom, I scrape all the old straw and manure from the floor of the hen house, then collect and place it on the compost. Cover it with soil. Sweep everything and add new straw. We never have rats. We had a rooster which upset the neighbours with his early morning crowing. Mother killed him.

In those days, people used to kill a chicken for Sunday lunch. It frightened me to see Mother chase the rooster and the terrible squawks as it died, and the bird jumped up and down without its head. It was worse for Mother, her face bright red with frustration. A big pot of boiled water bubbled on the stove, the dead bird dropped in. Then its feathers removed, and the degutting and finally, cooking the bird. Roast chicken for Sunday lunch took ages to prepare and was considered special.

Back to my day, a quick breakfast of toast and tea.

"Have some porridge or an egg," Mother said.

"No thanks." I never have an appetite in the morning. I leave for school.

After school, I do more chores. Mother has no time to go to the shops with the child minding.

"Can you please go to the shops for bread and more milk?" Mother asked.

This is a task I enjoy, as I drool over the sweets in the local milk bar. Sometimes the shopkeeper gives me a few free lollies in a tiny white bag.

Feed the chooks in the afternoon again and collect any eggs. Pull the downy brown feathers from the warm eggs. Close the pen later. Place the empty milk bottles out for the milkman. Polish my school shoes and do anyone else's shoes that need their shoes cleaning.

If I can manage to sneak off in a corner to read, I do. But often do not have the chance.

"Put down that book. Have you finished your homework?" Mother asked.

Start on my homework, later set the table in the warm kitchen with the aroma of a bubbling stew, or something equally as nice. The family sometimes has dinner in front of the television on collapsible TV trays. There was usually a mad panic to carry the trays into the kitchen if there was a surprise visit from someone from the church.

After the meal, I do the dishes or dive straight into my homework. If I manage to finish in time, I can watch a little TV.

Around 9.45 p.m., pack my school books and prepare the school uniform for the next day. Add the textbooks and homework into my satchel. Textbooks must be looked after as they must be sold at the end of each year. I cover the books in brown paper and clear plastic to protect them. They must be good as new. Once I sold a textbook to a student for four shillings and sixpence. I gave Mother the money, but she was furious as I had not asked her permission first.

"Wait until Jim comes home," she said glaring at me.

He was only five years older than me.

"Jim is not my father," I said, acting tough. "You

give him too much authority. He bosses me around all the time. He will boss you around soon. In fact, he does it now."

Now I am close to tears, run to my room.

"What about the other book?" Mother said, following behind.

It took me a while to understand; the other book belonged to John. I had borrowed the book for a school project on the Universe.

"Here it is," I said, handing the book.

She is still angry.

"It would be better if you dealt with me directly, for you are my mother. It would be better if you said, 'no TV for a week' or something like that. Instead of whacking me as I am older now," I said.

"I feel awful you know. You are looking after the children for money, my brothers working to support us, and I have not come top of the class to show you how hard I am trying at school...to make you proud of me..." I said.

Guilt my constant companion.

We make up. Mother said she will forget the whole thing.

Later, when pouring over my homework, Mother puts a cup of tea with an almond biscuit next to me. It is a truce of sorts.

Jim is good to us, even though I am annoyed about his bossiness toward me. He is young and trying to sort out his own life with girlfriends and mates and work. After my father's death, he and

John took on a more adult role in the family although they wanted to stay at school. When John left for farm work and later the army, Jim took the greater male role. Mother leans on him perhaps more than she should, brought up in a culture where the man is king.

Jim and I are pals most times. When he bought his old second-hand car, he took Mother and me on day trips and we visited places such as the Maroondah Dam and the Dandenongs.

The family problems started when Jim became seriously involved with his Australian girlfriend Jill and pulled away from us. Mother felt alienated and viewed Jill as the enemy.

To his credit, Jim did try to include us in some outings with Jill and she was nice to me. They had a passionate relationship and were often kissing, which upset Mother further. She would fume and say unkind words about Jill in Greek.

Jim is artistic and always drawing and paintings. He had real talent. If he did not have to leave school to support us, he might have concentrated on his art and would be a talented artist and become famous.

"Here, I bought you a square of carpet for your bedroom floor," Jim said one day.

He handed me a roll of carpet.

The flowery design made my room cheerful and felt warm on my feet, better than the floorboards. When Rosy came around later the same day she spilt tea on the rug. I mopped it carefully. The last thing I needed was to be part of more Mother dramas.

At night, I sometimes write to Chris, my penfriend who lives in England. We developed a friendship as pen pals. Her life's very different than mine. They have money and often go on holidays to exotic places like Italy and France. She attends an exclusive girl's school. Her writing is so small and cramped on the blue aerogram paper, it is hard to read. We share much about our lives; it is never specific, mostly about Australia or England customs or titbits about school.

I never mention any home conflict and certainly never write about Mother and her problems; instead, I discuss cheerful things and omit all the bad stuff.

CHAPTER 14

The Budgie

Springvale

1961

Jim has a friend who breeds budgies, and through him, brought home the blue budgie named Dennis. At first, Dennis was very timid, gradually became tame. I pride myself in teaching Dennis to talk. He says silly things thanks to me.

"Mummy, my little footsie's gone." He can say this so pitifully that it makes you laugh. The footsie refers to his foot. He often perches on one leg with the other in his feathers.

I taught him a little prayer, "Good night, pretty boy, God bless and keep you."

He likes to say "Jim, Jim," loudly.

Jim taught him to wolf whistle.

His main trick is to flutter his feathers and scatter the seeds around the cage and on the floor in the laundry. I clean his cage every day. If I am late taking his cover off his cage, he screeches at me and pulls threads off the cover. He does his morning exercise, stretches from his wings and feet. Knows how to make kissing noises like a human; little smacking noises.

Dennis is named after Dennis the Menace, a cartoon charter. He has become a part of the family and certainly acts as one of the family. He takes complete charge when he is let out of his cage and inspects what we are eating and if he likes it, will taste the food. He is a spoilt little budgie and rewards us with cheerful chattering. At one stage, we decided he might like a lady for company so organised a girl budgerigar called Cutie. At first, it looked as though they would not enjoy each other's friendship, but her shyness wore off and they became mates. They scratch and preen each other's feathers. When the budgies are on the swing together, one bends his head in the direction of the other who preens and scratches its feathers. They have arguments; you can hear that, loud raucous chirping, but only a few. The female budgie went through a crazy time where she would wash herself all the time. She looked funny with wet feathers, but that wore off.

Cutie is blue with a white head. Dennis is green with a yellow top. Dennis had been blue as a chick but when he moulted, he turned green and stayed like that ever since.

Some people suggest when you put a talking budgie in with another budgie, the talking stops and he adopts budgie language. But we proved them wrong. Before Dennis had a friend, he talked 'nineteen to the dozen' and still talks all the time.

Cutie has been with him for a year now, does not speak, and is not tame. Dennis lets me tickle him under his chin and stroke his feathers. He jumps on my outstretched finger when I open the cage door and travels on my shoulder chirping. Cutie would not dream of letting me do this.

I could go on forever.

Mother does not play with the budgies, looks out of the kitchen window for long periods of time picking at her lips and stares out into the garden.

"What are you looking at?" I asked and peer out of the window.

There is nothing there, only the lights of the neighbour's kitchen.

"Is something the matter?"

"I am thinking of Mr Woodrow," she said.

Mr Woodrow died on Tuesday of a blood vessel bursting in his brain. He was a neighbour, and for years he and his family lived on the corner opposite our house. He and his wife were good friends and supported for our family when my Father died. Mr Woodrow helped Mother deal with administrative and legal papers. At that time, we children were too young to know what to do and Mother had poor English. Mrs Woodrow became a friend to Mother and they stayed friends even though the Woodrows shifted to Kew.

"He was an upright man," she said silently. "Mrs Woodrow will miss him."

CHAPTER 15

Holidays

September 1963

Mrs Hicks was a large, friendly woman from our church. She fostered two dark-skinned Aboriginal sisters who had regular contact with their family.

"How lucky the girls are to be brought up as Christians," said one woman with pursed lips.

"I consider myself to be the lucky one, as I am part of the girls and their families," said Mrs Hicks.

The girls' family had fallen on hard times and they were placed in an orphanage. Mrs Hicks heard about them through a friend and asked to help and they came to stay with her. The father of the girls kept in contact with them; the mother left to be with her tribe up north.

Mrs Hicks had older children of her own, was a widow, and lived in a large house with a wide veranda that circled the house. The house was built on a large block with an impressive garden with peach, apple, apricot and orange trees. Mrs Hicks made jam with the fruit and bottled the rest in Fowlers Vacola jars. The supply of fruit lasted all year.

I loved playing with the sisters, although they

were younger than me and very shy. A doll's house lived on the veranda and was crafted by Mrs Hick's husband before he died. Each doll's house room was a replica of a room from a princess story with lace curtains and four poster beds. Miniature chandeliers hung from the ceiling. Small, painted doors opened and shut. Real carpet squares in the rooms and down the stairs. There was even a fountain in the front. The bathroom had a small porcelain bath and sink with miniscule taps over the sink. The kitchen had a stove, sink, and tiny taps. And a long table with chairs crafted from wood. The dolls had long hair that could be combed, were stitched by hand, and wore long Edwardian dresses in green and red velvet and had gold crowns on their heads.

I had never seen anything so beautiful in my life.

Mrs Hicks invited our family to join them on a camping adventure in the Dandenongs. Our family, Mother, Jim and I, and Mrs Hicks and her girls piled into her station wagon that was weighed down with camping equipment. It was my very first time camping. We stayed in two tents in the bush. Everyone scurried around and helped set up camp; some collected wood for the fire and others water from the stream. We followed directions on how to set up the tent. Spread a waterproof mat on the ground and set up the camp beds. I found it very exciting as it was all new to me. Mrs Hicks and her girls had camped many times before and were experts at setting up. Mother cooked chops and eggs over the campfire, which we ate heartily. Later we toasted bread over the fire and slathered strawberry jam over the toast.

We used gas lanterns at night, sat around the campfire, and told stories about the Australian bush, sang loud songs learnt from school, 'Once a jolly Swagman...' until our voices were hoarse.

This was our family's first time interacting with the Australian bush and we were surprised at how quiet it was, until the morning when the kookaburras called out, followed by a chorus by the magpies and currawongs. Young currawongs played near us; they ran feathered races with each other, rolled and played like children, preened each other's feathers. The baby currawongs were protected by the group and fed by all the adult birds. We stayed out of their area and watched.

A stream near us trickled over rocks where we washed dishes and swam in the cool waters.

Mrs Hicks's kindness to our family helped us cope with the loss of Father.

Another significant holiday; Mother, Jim and I, and budgie Dennis drove to Mildura for a holiday. The budgie came with us as we had no one to look after him. Cutie was not alive then. The plan was to drive to Mildura in Jim's second-hand car. Jim was nineteen; I was fourteen. The boot crammed with stuff we thought we might need. The family was innocent in every sense of the word and had no experience with what a road trip might entail.

We departed at 6 a.m., but still caught the morning traffic which slowed us down. By 8 a.m. were out of the Melbourne traffic and on our way to Mildura.

Jim was a thoughtful careful driver, handled the car well. Mother appeared happy. Dennis chattered and chirped and swung on his little green swing. I was jubilant; our big road trip. None of us had any idea of what was expected for such a holiday; no one made forward bookings for caravan parks. Every so often, Jim pulled the car over to a rest spot and we stopped for a cup of tea from the thermos and Mother's homemade cake.

The highway was not busy.

"Look out Jim, kangaroos," I shouted.

Two big, red kangaroos bounced over the road. This is the first time any of us have seen a real kangaroo. We are elated.

"They are so big," I said.

"I would hate to crash into one," said Jim.

Mother was wide-eyed.

By lunchtime, we passed Bendigo and knew we were one-third of the way to Mildura.

"This is a big adventure," said Jim.

I agreed; we had never travelled so far from home.

By 4 p.m., Jim and Mother were tired, so at Sea Lake, we searched for a place to stay. We tried a few hotels with no success. Eventually found two rooms at the Railway hotel. Mother, Budgie and me in one room and Jim had the other room. The place had showers, which we needed as we were dusty, and slept like logs.

The next day we set off early; by lunch-time arrived in Mildura. Tried every caravan park in Mildura but they had no vacancies. Cruised around feeling foolish, eventually located the Tourist Information Centre.

"Only private caravans are available," said the woman at the Information Centre.

She wrote the address for a Mrs Paul who had a caravan to rent.

The caravan was new, large and luxurious, and parked in their driveway.

"We planned a dream holiday around Australia," said Mrs Paul, "but Mr Paul became ill." She eyed us curiously. Dennis chirped encouragement. We were not the usual tourists, a shy Greek woman, teenage son and daughter, and a bird in a cage.

"You have a budgie," she said, a little surprised at Dennis's whistling.

"We had no one to look after Dennis," I said. "He is part of the family, we couldn't leave him behind."

"Anyone who loves their pets is fine with me," Mrs Paul said.

We sighed with relief, planned to stay a week. The rental cost fifteen pounds, fifteen shillings, and included the use of the caravan's gas cooker and beds. The outside shower and toilet were within walking distance. The caravan had curtains, stove, fridge, cupboards, a double bed which Mother and I slept on, and a smaller bed that Jim used, which became a table during the day. The caravan still had a new smell about it. Dennis chirped his approval.

The next day made plans to visit Wentworth and the Darling River and check the old jail. The cells in the jail had no bars, only a small gap high up for windows. This was a depressing place with a steel contraption that the prison officers could open and peek at the prisoners. We climbed up the top to the watchtower; a nice view for the prison officers.

Mildura is mainly an agricultural city, the focus on grapes and citrus fruit. It is modern and has many shops. We visited Lake Cullulleraine where many people cooked meat on barbeques. The smell of the cooked meat made us hungry.

"I think we're lost," said Jim at one stage.

Stared down an empty road, we had been sightseeing and took the wrong turn off. We drove around and around trying to find our way back. Our map was old and out of date.

Mother's face creased into a frown.

Sometime later Jim found a familiar track and we made it back to the caravan.

Jim and I walked to the local fish and chips and bought crispy fried flakes, three dim Sims, and chips for tea. It felt like a feast. The caravan table perfect for the three of us and Dennis sat on my shoulder.

"How are you doing?" said Mr Paul.

Some days he looked frail and had difficulty walking even with his walking stick. He gave us advice on the best places to visit in Mildura and how to get there.

"What is Lesvos like?" he asked one day.

"It had been a dream of my wife and me to visit Greece one day," he said. "Now that is not possible." He looked sad.

"What happened to your father?" he asked.

Jim told him. He and Jim had developed a friendship. I think Mr Paul was lonely.

One day he knocked on the caravan door, "Would you like to come inside and hear the piano music I composed?" he said.

Of course, we did.

The three of us trooped into the lounge room, the piano room had long, red velvet drapes and flower-patterned carpet, a large wooden bookcase full of books, long oblong table with chairs. It seemed very elegant to me.

Mr Paula's piano playing was faultless. He lifted his fingers over the keyboard and played without sheet music. He played a few pieces and we asked for more. Mrs Paul beamed encouragement and offered us homemade Anzac biscuits.

We clapped enthusiastically. "That was wonderful," we said.

Their backyard had a thriving vegetable garden

of beans, tomatoes, lettuces and cauliflower and flowering shrubs and roses.

"Do you use fertilizer on your plants?" Mother asked Mrs Paul one day.

I was surprised. Mother was normally worried about speaking English with strangers.

"I use chicken manure and compost," said Mother.

"So do I," said Mrs Paul.

"Mr Paul doesn't do any gardening now; he is too sick with cancer. I do all the work," she said, looking downcast.

"I will say a prayer and light a candle for you both," said Mother, and reached out to pat her arm.

Mrs Paul knocked on the caravan door the next day.

"These are for you. I picked beans, tomatoes and lettuce; hope you can use them," she said.

Mother was pleased and shared our almond cakes from home with her.

Another day Mrs Paul lent us copies of *The Woman's Weekly,* which we read from cover to cover.

Each day, the three us planned excursions and explored different parts of Mildura. Our routine after breakfast was to tidy and go. Mother made sandwiches and filled the thermos for a picnic lunch. We ate grilled chops or sausages with vegetables and salad for the evening meal. The caravan stove worked well.

At the end of the week, we were sorry to leave

Mr and Mrs Paul; they had been wonderful to us and very generous.

Mother and I spent the morning cleaning the caravan; it was spotless when we left.

"Thank you for looking after us; we loved staying here," said Jim.

"I prayed for you to get well," Mother said to Mr Paul.

"Safe trip home," said Mr and Mrs Paul. Their brown cocker spaniels nudged us for final pats.

Onward and forward to Echuca.

On the way to Nyam, we had our first Aussie barbeque with sausages and onions in a bread bun at the barbeque area next to the river. We even had sweet tasting billy tea.

Now we were real Australians.

The caravan park at Echuca was a disappointment; old, rundown and cramped, but had a wonderful view of the Murray River, smooth and peaceful. Echuca was a major port and I envisaged the past with steamboats moving up and down the river.

Magpies and currawongs serenaded us on our evening river walk.

"This is lovely," said Mother, a peaceful look on her face.

Jim and I glanced at each other and grinned.

Mother seemed happy for the first time in a long time.

The next day we drove over the metal bridge into New South Wales, purchased half a case of oranges and grapefruit. The oranges were sweet and full of juice; we ate two each and planned to take the rest home.

"Any fruit?" asked the fruit inspector on our return to the Victorian side of the bridge.

We had been eating oranges; he spotted the half case on the floor.

"The law states you cannot bring fruit over the border to Victoria because of fruit flies. You have to hand the fruit to us." The man said.

He wore a uniform and hat and a very stern expression on his face.

"Or face a heavy fine."

"That's not fair," Jim said.

"The law is the law," the fruit inspector said and took the case of fruit.

"We wasted our money." Mother was furious.

Friday, we set off for home, only stopping for another barbeque on the way, sausages in bread this time.

Home at last. It was good to be home; I missed our home.

Mother looked weary, Dennis survived. Jim's old car made it, and Jim was a safe and wonderful driver.

Jim, Mother, Dennis, and I were now real Australians having experienced a road trip and barbeque.

The memory of this holiday stands out like a shining sapphire in my young life.

The black-and-white photos show a happy group.

CHAPTER 16

Engagements

Springvale

1964

Our lives changed rapidly when Jim and Jill became engaged. Her parents held a big engagement party at their house. We were all invited including John's then-finance Angela and her Mother. It was a chance for the two families to know each other. We were very excited; at least I was. A hairdresser came to our house with her hair dryer and washed and set all the women's hair. John paid for it.

The engagement party was a fancy affair. A buffet table crammed with plates of food, another table for sweets, and another for alcohol and other drinks. A band played rock 'n' roll music, which was perfect for dancing. Strobe-coloured lights flashed different colours over the dancers. People laughed and danced. I wore a pink dress with a wide swish skirt that Mother had made and white high heels and felt grown up. One of Jill's relatives asked me for a dance; I think he was put up to it. Both of us nervous and improvised our rock 'n' roll steps. Mother sat with the women and looked unhappy.

"My wife and I welcome Jim and his family into our family," said Jill's Father.

He was a tall, fair-haired man; his short wife had auburn hair.

The room exploded in wolf whistles, cheers, and claps.

"I am grateful for your welcome and for raising such a beautiful daughter. I will cherish her always," said Jim.

Jim always knew the right thing to say.

Mother tried to mix with the others but felt overwhelmed, although everyone was kind and chatted with her.

~

But it was not to last; Mother continued her bombardment of Jim.

"Jill is not good enough for you," she said shaking her finger at him. "Mark my words; she will not be a good wife to you. She can't even cook or sew."

"I don't care what you say; I love Jill," he said.

"Anyway, it is my life, and I will do what I want," he said. "Why can't you be like Jill's Mother and Father and accept us?"

Mother muttered something rude in Greek.

The arguments went on for weeks, the final straw came when Mother made him choose between her and Jill.

"I love you and Mother," he said to me before he left.

I was in my room, face swollen and ugly from crying.

"Please don't go," I said. "Mother is sick and doesn't understand what she is saying."

"I have to leave for my own sanity. I can't live with things the way they are with Mother," Jim said.

"I promise to keep in touch and you can ring me at work."

We had no phone. The nearest phone was in the phone box a street away.

So, he left. He rented a small room near his work. He did not leave in a huff, but in a quiet, detached manner, leaving me mortified and upset. I was shocked. Nothing I could say would change his mind.

Mother acted tough; I think she must have cried later. She had no idea of the extent of Jim's love for Jill and thought she could push him to break off with Jill.

Her mental state became worse and was destroying the family.

Sometime after Jim left, I received a letter from Angela to say that she and John were no longer engaged. Again, I was upset and sad. Mother loved Angela and thought her perfect for John.

Jim and Jill were still engaged, and Mother hated that idea.

Angela said that John was to leave for active duty in Malaysia with the Australian army. He had fears of being killed as it was a dangerous mission and felt it would be unfair to Angela if they were engaged and he was killed. They decided to wait until he returned from Malaysia. It didn't make sense to me.

John came to stay with us before his deployment to Malaysia. During that time, John and Mother argued continuously. He tried every way he could to tell her that the voices and perceived persecution were not real. It was in her head. But she refused to hear.

In desperation, he said to me, "You must help Mother move from this place. She is mentally sick and needs to get away. Help her find employment as a cook somewhere far away."

"How can I do this?" I asked, scared of the prospect.

"You will find a way; you are smart," he said.

John always said that when he didn't know the answer himself.

John left for Malaysia; we don't know if we would ever see him again. I studied the war and was terrified. John could be killed. Indonesia started the war when it launched a series of cross-border raids into Malaysian territory. The newspapers and television were full of the conflict. I held my breath whenever it was mentioned. The war lasted from 1962-1966 and was initially between Indonesia and Malaysia. Somehow troops from Australia,

New Zealand, and Britain became involved. Many Australian soldiers were killed and injured.

I thought of John in the swamps of Malaysia and prayed he wouldn't be killed.

~

John is gone. So is Jim. It is just me now and Mother and her paranoia.

She hears the voices and they demand she do more and more strange things. She lies on the floor with a rug. The voices told her. She paces day and night, picking her lips and muttering. She shouts defiance at the voices and to the world outside.

I am stuck at home with her and am afraid.

CHAPTER 17

Mother and her growing paranoia

Springvale

1964 and 1965

Mother's mental illness is making my life miserable. She thinks almost everyone in the world is against her. Believes people hide and whistle at her specifically. If we are down the street and she hears someone happy and whistling, she turns around and mutters nasty things in Greek.

"Shut up, leave me alone," she then shouts in English.

I hate it, am on eggshells all the time in case something sets her off.

"There is a conspiracy out there and people are out to harm me," Mother said.

"Who wants to harm you, and why?" I asked.

She does not answer.

"We should see a doctor; you are not sleeping properly," I said.

"There is nothing wrong with me; it is the persecutors that are wrong," she said.

"The voices are not real," I said. "No one can hear them except you. I can't hear them."

She ignores me.

I ring Jim at work and ask for his help.

"There is nothing I can do," he said.

John is in Malaysia.

Every so often as though out of a sleep, she becomes my proper Mother again and is loving and caring. I don't relax as I know it will not last. Something always sets her off and she turns into a mad woman.

It feels hopeless. Her mental illness affected Jim, her favourite child, and caused him to leave home. It affected John as he tried to reason with her. But he could not. I tried reasoning with her and tried to get medical help.

My friends who are the same age as me, sixteen, have such happy lives with parties, boyfriends. But not me. They have so much, and I have so little.

Financially it is difficult. We struggle to manage on Mother's widow pension.

"I could get a part-time job," I said.

"No, I will not allow it; you have to concentrate on your school work," she said.

"But I want to help," I said.

"Don't argue with me; I am your Mother," she said.

Mother doesn't look after the small children anymore. I am not sure why. John sends some money for my education and the pressure is on me to get great marks.

Who can I tell? How can I get help? I am a just a teenager with no status or power. I tried to talk to the local doctor, it did no good. Sometimes the pressure is so heavy on me I can barely breathe.

I pour over library books about psychology to try to learn anything that can help. Nothing works; Mother needs psychiatric medicine, but she refuses. Mother is sick and all I can do is pray.

~

Mother has agreed to leave Springvale and to take John's advice and create some distance from the neighbourhood and the seeds of her mental illness. Not sure where. I loathe the thought of saying goodbye to my friends.

Each day is a drag, long and hopeless.

I win a Matriculation bursary to study but must give it up as Mother said I must leave school and go wherever she goes.

Mother and I scanned the newspapers for a position as Housekeeper. We found one for a group of priests in Fish Creek. Mother felt she would be at peace working for men of God. The job seemed perfect. Fish Creek is a long distance from here and the conspiracy issues for Mother and there is a high school nearby, so I could do my matriculation there. I wrote the application.

The priest visited us, perhaps to check us out.

"I am sorry, but the position has been filled," he said.

Perhaps he recognised Mother had problems.

I wrote an ad in the local newspaper to rent our house, but no luck.

We are all stressed. Jim told me he is so upset he needs pills to sleep.

I cannot cope with the strain of Mother's mental illness. With Jim and John gone, I am left alone to deal with her weird behaviours and madness. Nothing I do works; nothing I do helps. I am two people, the person at home with my mad mother, and the person trying to live in the real world.

Occasionally Mother and I catch up with Jim and Jill. He bought us tickets to the movie *My Fair Lady* and we all saw it together. It was the most wonderful movie I had ever seen; the music and costumes transported me to another world. Jim and Jill had tea at our place and left, and for once no one fought.

This week Jim visited by himself; Mother and he had a huge fight. They screamed at each other until he slammed the door and left.

John is in Malaysia and cannot write as he is on patrol. Now and then Angela gets a note from him and she writes and tells us the news.

I cannot sleep with worry. I hear the milkman and his horse clomping along the road as he delivers milk. Have become a night owl, write and read until the small hours of the morning until I fall asleep exhausted.

Mother walks up and down the corridor shouting at the voices all night.

I won a teaching bursary; this will help with my education.

It is the start of the school year; all the students in my year twelve class have started back at school. But I am not at school. We are moving but where? Am sad, I want to do the Matriculation with my friends. But it is not going to happen.

Eventually, Mother is successful in obtaining a position as a cook at Kaniva Hospital. I must go with her. It is a terrifying thought and fills me with dread.

I draft a letter to the Matron at Kaniva Hospital. 'Mother and I accept your kind offer for a position as cook at Kaniva Hospital. I hope to attend the local high school and would like a part-time job at the hospital after school and on weekends. I am happy to wash dishes or do anything that is required.'

Sadly, they only have correspondence courses for Matriculation students at Kaniva High School; only a few subjects are available.

Mother complains and moans. She is getting on my nerves. I am giving up so much for her, but she refuses to see any of it. I am so angry and have my suspicions that moving to faraway Kaniva will not do anything for her mental state. In fact, I suspect it will become worse.

Another letter arrives from the Matron at Kaniva Hospital, they have a part-time job available for me setting up and collecting patients' food trays and doing the dishes. We start work in March.

Mother refused to tell Jim we are moving. Her secrecy drives me nuts.

Eventually, Mother informed Jim about the new job in Kaniva the week before we are due to leave. Jim will move back home to look after the house, so we do not need to rent it.

The day of our departure, Jim drove us to the station. We caught every red light on the way. Jim's petrol tank ran dry. Luckily, he carried a little extra fuel with him. We reached Spencer Street station ten minutes before the train was due to leave.

At the station, I sobbed into Jim's chest.

"You will be okay sis; take good care of Mother," he said.

His voice tapered off and I could see his lips quiver.

Mother was stony-faced, said nothing, still blamed Jim for the fact we had to leave as she believed he was in league with the conspirators. The voices had told her this information.

We found our carriage, throw our bags in.

"Where are you off to?" asked a pleasant woman in our carriage.

I told her.

"Kaniva is a nice friendly town; I live in Horsham, but my sister lives in Kaniva. I go there often. You and your Mother will love it there." She said.

I was not convinced.

We changed trains at Dimboola, caught the small wagon train to Kaniva, arrived at 5:45 p.m., tired and hungry. It has been blistering hot, my dress soaked with sweat.

Mother sat quietly hardly speaking the whole journey. She had shrunk and now looked small and vulnerable. How will she cope with cooking for a hospital of patients and staff? My heart went out to her.

"We will be all right," I said in Greek. "God will look after us."

She crossed herself. "I hope so," she said.

I could see the strain was affecting her deeply.

What was she thinking? I wish I knew.

The matron met us at Kaniva station and drove us to the hospital. She showed us our rooms in the nursing home quarters. The rooms were very small: a bed, a desk and dressing table, and a small cupboard. Matron left a vase of red carnations in our rooms as a welcome; this was a nice gesture. We were ushered into the kitchen for an overview of the work to be done.

The relief cook showed us around.

CHAPTER 18

Kaniva Hospital

Kaniva

March 1965

I learnt that Kaniva is located on the Western Highway, north of Little Desert National Park. It has a small population, about 900. The town is a rest point for those travelling to Adelaide. Surrounding Kaniva are vast wheat fields and sheep stations, which have flourished since the late 1800s.

The next day I enrolled at Kaniva High School and met the other two students doing Matriculation by correspondence. Graham is short and dark, smart and into science. Harvey does humanities and is gentle. Both come from farming backgrounds and have lived in the area all their lives.

The subjects that are available are Geography, Modern History, British History, English Literature, and English. I am dreading correspondence school.

For some strange reason, I am a curiosity at the school. The students are friendly; the questions come thick and fast.

"Why did you come here?" they ask.

Tell them little except that Mother has a job at the hospital and I must go with her.

The three of us in the matriculation class are provided with a small room for us to work on our correspondence work. The mail brings large packages of typed material for us to read and complete. An English teacher occasionally helps. Otherwise, it is up to us to work- or not.

After school, I race to the hospital, set the trays for the evening meal and take them out with the steaming soup and meal to the patients. Later collect and wash the dishes.

Mother cooks all day with a short break in between meals. She shows signs of stress and is hot and flustered. I help her where I can, such as ordering meat and vegetables and other supplies as her English is not good. But her cooking is perfect. She prepares delicious meals which the patients, staff, and matron rave about.

"What are you cooking today, Mrs E?" A nurse asked, filling up a glass of water.

Mother mentions a roast or casserole or whatever.

"Yum, make sure the patients don't eat it all. Please leave me some," said the nurse.

One night we are invited to see a movie with the matron. It is a nice distraction. The white-haired matron is fierce with her nurses but kind to us. I notice her hands shake; she takes medication, probably for Parkinson's.

One day the matron asks me to translate for a Greek woman who about to give birth in the maternity part of the hospital. She and her husband cannot speak English. I stay in the birthing room with the Greek woman from the start of the patient's labour to the birth.

"Push," I said in Greek.

"The doctor said to push hard now."

"Puff, the doctor said to puff."

Sometime later a baby girl is born, and I am struck dumb with the miracle aspects of the birth. To me, it is magical, surreal. I decide there and then to be a nurse and forget about teaching. The parents named the baby after me and were grateful for my presence.

I was on a high all day and had never experienced anything so special in my life.

Harvey and I caught a train to Dimboola for a Vocational Guidance session. It felt as if I had stepped back in history. The streets and buildings are very Old World, federation buildings with columns and steps. Dimboola sits on the Wimmera River and was home to the Wotjobaluk Aboriginal people until the first European settlers arrived. They tell me that the district was known as 'Nine Creeks' because of the many little streams that appear when the river recedes after floods.

Graeme had his life planned, his goal to study science at Melbourne University, and did not need vocational guidance.

Mr Brownhill, the Headmaster, made me Prefect and I felt quite honoured. I helped with the school social, assisted in decorating the hall. The social was joyful, and I danced with many boys. It reminded me of the socials at Springvale High School. One young chap took a shine to me and even asked me out. But I said no. Mother would never give permission to go out on a date.

In between, I received letters from my friends at Springvale High telling me of the gossip. Missed them all and wanted to be with them.

The Headmaster encouraged me to enter a public speaking contest, which to my surprise I won. This meant I had to catch a train to speak in Horsham. My speech discussed the differences between my old school and 1,000-plus students and three of us doing Matriculation by correspondence. The speech featured in *The Weekly Times* newspaper.

Jim drove to see us Kaniva in his new black Volkswagen car, a Beetle—his pride and joy. We loved seeing him, had a picnic in the forest near the hospital. He told us he and Jill were no longer engaged. The conflict between Mother and Jim had ended. Apparently, Mother was right; Jill was not the right girl for Jim. He stayed at the railway hotel and we ate there with him at night.

Sadly, as I predicted, Mother's paranoia manifested itself again, and she felt the conspirators had followed her to Kaniva and were again whispering and talking about her. Mother muttered to the voices under breath in the day as she worked in the kitchen. And spoke loudly to the voices in her room at night.

"Leave me alone," she said to no one visible to me.

During the final exams, I fainted due to lack of sleep trying to fit in study and work every night.

Mother resigned from the cooking position when John notified us he had finished his tour of duty in Malaysia and was coming home.

Despite my initial fears and trepidation, I enjoyed my time in Kaniva, made some friends, and developed confidence. Although my education had been uneven due to the correspondence lessons, I have warm memories of Kaniva.

And I grew up.

The next year commenced my nursing training at the Alfred Hospital. It turned out to be an excellent career move.

And returned to teaching as an academic at University several years later.

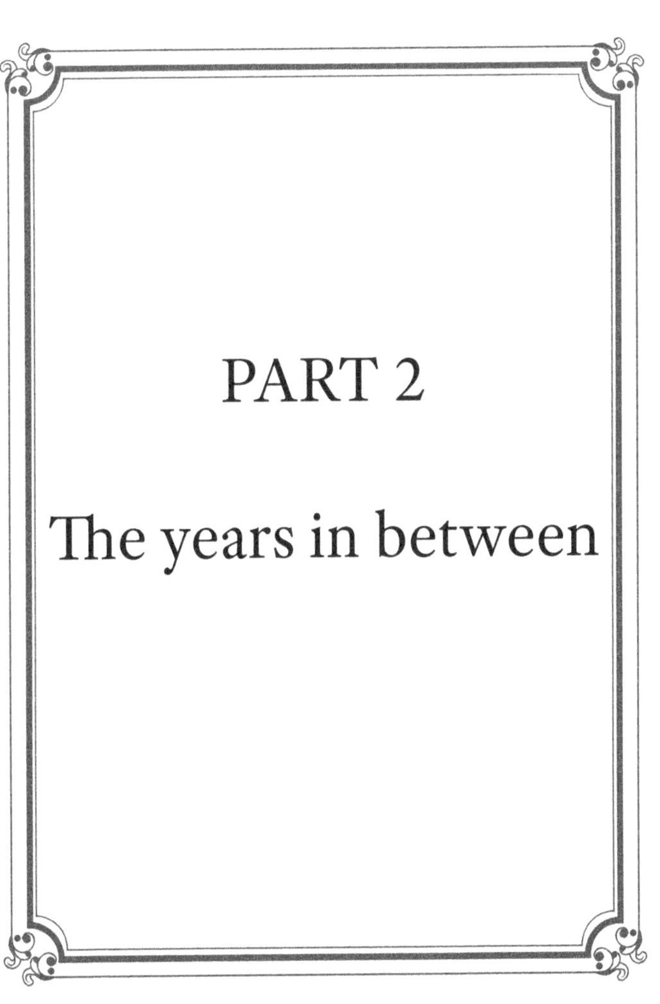

PART 2

The years in between

CHAPTER 19

The years in between

Our family

1966 and beyond

Before he died, Father spoke of his passionate dream to run a small farm. He drew elaborate plans for the garden, showing where the animals and trees would be.

"I want to build a small farm, so we can be self-sufficient," he said to us at the dinner table.

The plans for the farm spread in front of him.

"The orchard will be here. We will have peach, pear, and orange trees."

He pointed these out on his plan.

"The vegetables here, we can make enough to sell. And..." he turned to me.

"We will have a horse for Cally and calves for Mother to teach to suck and look after."

"John will study at Dookie Agricultural College and Jim at art school and Cally wherever she wants."

It was the family's dream goals. We talked about it often. There were times when we felt the dream could become a reality, really believed it in our hearts.

He died before the dream became a reality.

In 1966, John was back from the Malaysian conflict and Jim at loose ends and keeping in mind Mother's problems, they combined their money and placed a deposit on a small house and country property at Taggerty at the base of Cradle Mountain.

It was decided not to sell the Springvale house; instead rented it to an American couple who were delighted to have a garden.

I started nursing at the Alfred Hospital. On longer breaks from work, I would catch a bus to Taggerty. It was beautiful, Cradle Mountain creating a lovely background for the farm. Early morning the mist would cover the mountain and it would look mystical and mysterious. When the sun shone, the mountain stood strong and powerful. The small house had a wood stove and was simple. But the garden was transformed into masses of vegetables and flowers by Mother's magical hands.

My brothers bought calves, and as Father had wanted Mother taught them to suck and drink milk.

It was a happy time for them at the farm with the spirit of Father's dream in the background. Mother's mental illness had settled down to some mutterings to the voices.

My brothers and Mother worked extraordinary long hours making the place profitable.

I loved the place. But when the recession came, money dried up; the farm had to be sold.

It was heartbreaking for all. The family felt that they had ruined Father's dream.

It was decided that John and Jim would take Mother with them when they moved to Adelaide to find work.

In South Australia, Mother lived with my brothers until they married.

She then moved to a retirement village in Modbury.

Mother became upset that every time the aged pension increased; it was followed immediately by a rental increase by the retirement village.

"This is not right," she said.

Mother decided to fight the increase. She knocked on the doors of each unit at the Modbury village, collected signatures from the residents who were furious about the increases. A friend of Mother's typed a letter from all the residents. This letter was delivered to the Anglican Church Housing Trust who owned the retirement village. They were surprised at the gall of this small European lady. After consideration, the rental was capped for a year for all the units.

I have the letter from the Anglican Church Housing Trust detailing their response to her letter and signatures.

While in Modbury, Mother was active in Meals on Wheels, the Red Cross, and a church group.

Although my brothers and Mother lived in South Australia, we kept regular contact and I and my family would bus, drive, or fly to Adelaide. I was worried about Mother and her mental illness. At one stage, her mental state became worse and she lost any sense of reality, screamed in terror because of her hallucinations. I was a nurse and knew what had to be done. Mother was certified as an involuntary patient and admitted into a psychiatric hospital. She spent some time there and received medication that quieted the voices.

My brothers John and Jim married and had children of their own.

Jim married a Greek girl Sofia, and John, like me, married an Australian. Her name was Helen.

Mother loved my brothers' wives and children and they, in turn, adored her.

Sadly, her mental health issues became worse again and she begged to live with me in Victoria as the voices had become frightening again.

During those years, I had completed my nursing at The Alfred Hospital in Prahran, met and married Alan, and had two children, David and Cath. We lived in Sunbury for a while and then moved to Bullengarook where we also indulged our dream of a hobby farm with chickens, ducks, extensive fruit trees, and lambs. The children attended the local community schools and we were happy. This changed in 1987 when son Dave was badly injured in a motor vehicle accident. Dave required a long and complicated rehabilitation from broken bones and severe head injuries which changed his and our lives forever.

Mother came to live with us at Bullengarook in a Granny flat on our property. Her connection with nature legendary, her green fingers transformed every place she lived into a luxurious garden. At Bullengarook she planted fruit trees, vegetables, and flowers, and made African violets sing. Her granny flat festooned with twenty pots of dizzy-coloured African violets that were grown from leaf cuttings. She propagated almond trees from cuttings which grew to be fruitful.

While in Bullengarook, Mother became active in the local church and elderly citizens groups. Mother had a special friend, Mrs Morrison, who at eighty rode her horse Spike to visit my mother. The horse was tied to a tree while the two ladies enjoyed Greek cakes and hot tea. At the end of the visit, Mrs Morrison would climb on her horse and ride to Waterloo Road clutching a bag of homemade Greek cakes for later.

Mother was an extraordinary cook, made magnificent Greek and Australian food. She excelled in special treats for her grandchildren. Dave and Cath remember the piles of special cakes and pancakes she made just for them. Her Sunday roasts were legendary, cooked in the Greek way with lemon and rosemary.

Unfortunately, her mental illness came back, and she was admitted several times when life became unbearable because of the voices.

~

Mother cared for those less fortunate than herself. I remember driving through Melbourne city with her, we saw an old man rummaging through a rubbish bin looking for scraps of food.

"Stop the car," she said.

"Give that poor hungry man money for food. I remember only too well the feelings of hunger during the war."

I pulled over and handed the startled man money for food.

"Thanks, lady," he said.

I could smell alcohol on his breath. Whether he spent the money on alcohol or food I will never know.

Mother sewed beautiful clothes in a professional manner, cutting patterns for dresses from brown paper; she knitted and crotcheted. She always had something on the go for the grandchildren—a jumper, a top, a poncho. My children and my brother's children adored their Nana E.

Alan's mother also was loved by our children; was called Nanna B.

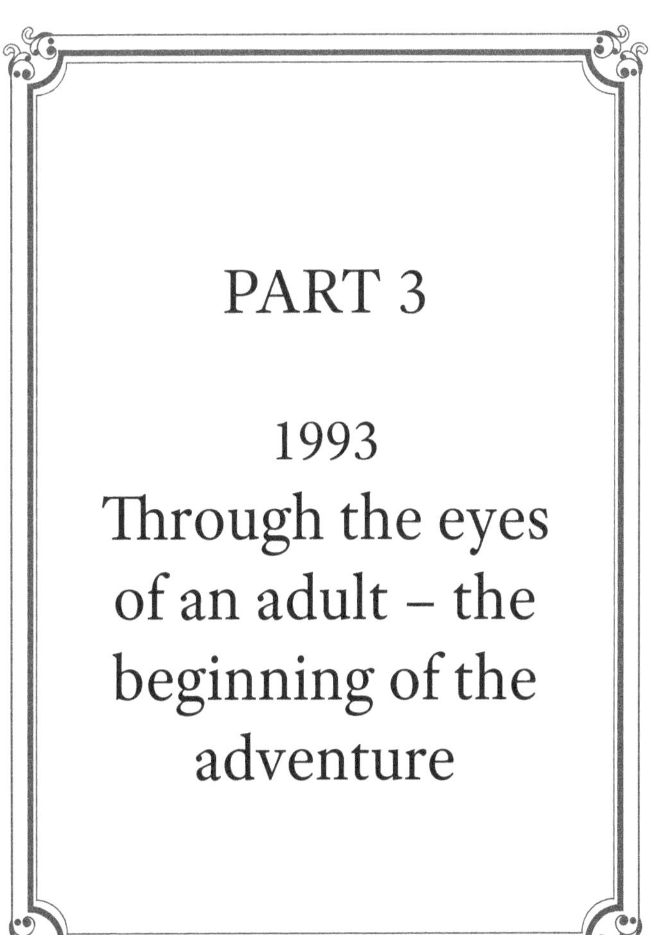

PART 3

1993
Through the eyes of an adult – the beginning of the adventure

CHAPTER 20

The beginning of the adventure

June 1993

The atmosphere in the aircraft cabin is one of high spirits. The three of us—Mother, husband Alan and I—are secured in the economy section of the plane, seated three abreast in the middle. Mother elegant, dressed in her good grey, wool dress which matches her silver hair, a silk blue scarf knotted loosely around her neck.

"So many people..." she said, her face glowing with excitement. She glances left and right. The sensory bombardment of men and women and children marching past, noise, unfamiliarity is hard for her to take in. She fidgets, is out of her comfort zone.

"We will have a wonderful time," I said and squeeze her hand.

I hope this is true.

A group of elderly ladies from Gwenap, where Mother currently lives, came to see her off at the airport. They arrived in a small bus with their walkers and frames, accompanied by a nurse. This is a treat for the oldies to go to the airport and see one of their residents at the airport. Mother has the status of being the only Gwenap oldie to fly internationally.

"You are so lucky to be going on a holiday to Greece," they said.

"Yes, I know," Mother said.

Mother and her friends had tea and cake and waved Mother off like a movie star.

A river of people continues to jostle down the aircraft, laden with bags and coats. They scramble for seats, open and bang shut overhead lockers, check follow passengers before sitting and clicking the seat buckles. One baby has already started screaming.

Alan adjusts everything, retrieves his book. I stand up and take in the plane.

Earlier, I had spotted friend Frieda at the airport, travelling to England to meet up with family. She is on the same plane, sitting in the row ahead of us.

It is 2:30 p.m. What time in Greece? I don't do the math.

Daughter Cath came to see us off at Melbourne airport. Son sent his good wishes.

Brothers John and Jim rang last night from Adelaide.

"Have a wonderful time," said John. "I know you will," he said.

"Take care," said Jim.

I was four when we left Lesvos in 1952, John was

eleven, Jim nine. They remember much more about life there than I do. Jim thought the trip a bad idea initially but relented. He thought Mother's age and health would be too much for her to travel so far. John thought it a wonderful idea and contributed money for Mother's ticket.

In Australia, John became a staunch Aussie, even changed his surname from the Greek Evangelou to Evans. But last night when he rang, he relayed stories I had not heard before; somehow our trip has opened the past for him.

"I remember playing at the old Castle in Mytilene with friends. I was hit on the head by a falling rock." John said.

As a rule, John never mentions his childhood in Mytilene.

The flight attendants continue to point passengers to seats, smile, make small talk, and smile again. They are immaculately made up, a whiff of Channel No. 5 wafts past as one passes. I hear them talking to each other.

"Where did you have hair done? It looks different," said one.

"The hairdresser at the airport," said the other.

I crane my neck to see the flight attendant's hair. It is sleek and in a roll at the back of her head, heavily sprayed and blonde elegance.

It is just another day for them, but to us, it is the most exciting day of our lives.

Seats buckled, safety drill.

"Where are the exits?" I ask Alan.

"Weren't you paying attention to the safety drill?"

I admit I wasn't listening, too distracted with the thrill that we were going back to Lesvos, the island of my birth.

The plane makes a roaring noise, we taxi, take off. We are in the belly of what sounds like a giant vacuum cleaner. Hold Mother's hand. Alan closes his eyes, is a seasoned traveller. And calm as a cucumber. I close my eyes. My emotions running riot in my head. How will I manage? I practice the Greek alphabet in my head, alpha, beta, gamma... get stuck halfway. Scribble the Greek letters to calm me down.

It will be all right, I tell myself to self-soothe. I hate the moment when the plane dips and tilts to one side and the skyline is sloped. Close my eyes but feel the changes. When it straightens up, breathe again, and stop tensing.

Have started a travel journal of sorts; plan to capture every experience in an exercise book, to remember this trip of a lifetime. It is hard to write as the plane is shaking. Try to distract Mother by talking about the trip. There is turbulence, we are bounced around, the seatbelts anchor us to the seats. Alan reads, is nonplussed.

Mr Bean is on the movie channel. The plane erupts in laughter at something Mr Bean has done. Plane journeys force strangers to be together for the flight. An intimacy of sorts, we are all foreigners bunched together in this metal tube called a plane. A dishevelled man with long, strange hair and wearing a blue beanie and orange jumpsuit. He staggers down the aisle to the toilets. Is he a religious man or someone weird? A man near me retrieves a corkscrew from the overhead locker. I watch him open his duty-free liquor and take a swig from the bottle.

We bump and shake more turbulence. I adjust the new travel pouch bag still clipped to my waist under my shirt. It holds our plane tickets, traveller's cheques, money, and my American Express card. Cannot afford to lose it. I pat it periodically to make sure it is there. Mother's medicines are stored in my hand luggage in case the other suitcase is lost in transit.

Years ago, I promised Mother I would take her back to Mytilene. Mother is now old and needs much help. Will it be worthwhile? We are both excited about the idea of going to Mytilene. Alan less so, but he is tagging along to help. It has cost me a lot in time and money. I had to apply for special leave, sort out my work, organise a replacement lecturer for my classes, and obtain a personal loan from the credit union to pay for everything. I am exhausted. I have been running around in circles for weeks getting everything ready. Working until late every night; preparing, teaching, marking, everything perfect for my students and replacement lecturer. I have not had time to get excited about the trip. I hope it will be worthwhile.

We are calling our trip The Odyssey, returning to Mytilene, Lesvos after forty-two years away. This is our big adventure. I have talked and planned this trip for months, decades if you count the earlier plans made as a child. Have made no specific day-to-day plans, perhaps do a little sightseeing and return home. I carry a manila folder containing three of my Father's old letters written in Greek, a small plan of our old house in Thyra Street, and several black-and-white aging photos.

Had peculiar dreams for weeks of an elderly, white-haired man calling me to come to Greece. What does it mean? Who is the old man in my dream? No one I know. Perhaps my imagination is playing tricks.

The drink trolley comes, Mother, Alan, and I sip champagne. The three of us lift our glasses and toast our trip.

"A toast to our adventure," I said.

"To our adventure," said Mother and Alan clinking glasses.

The alcohol goes to my head and I feel dizzy. I shouldn't be drinking alcohol on an empty stomach. Mother nods off to sleep oblivious to the drone of the aeroplane.

Crane my neck to peer out to the windows;

only blue sky. Where are we? No idea. I am in a plane suspended in thin air. It feels ridiculous. Any moment the plane could drop like a stone to the ground. Despite knowing the science of aerodynamics of flight, my brain reasons otherwise and never lets me sleep on planes no matter how I try. My subconscious stays awake and blurts out missiles of fear. Am envious of those that can sleep and can wake refreshed.

Frieda comes, and we catch up on the gossip.

"I nearly didn't make it to the airport," Frieda said. "I couldn't find my ticket. Searched high and low and then found it sitting on the bench under a book," she said.

The baby is screaming again. Pressurisation is painful for babies.

The plane journey is long, bone-shaking weariness and being squashed into tiny seats in economy doesn't help. When the man in front of my seat extends his seat over my space, I am appalled. My tiny space has shrunk further.

"Can you please move your seat forward a little?" I said in a pleasant voice.

He mumbles something rude.

I call the flight attendant and she tells him to move his seat up as the meals will be handed out soon. He moves his seat forward, turns and glares at me.

Every so often, I walk Mother up and down the aisle to the toilet and to prevent blood clots.

Make sure she has her medicine and eye drops at the appropriate times, give adequate fluids. Sleep deprivation and time zone changes can play havoc with anyone, especially old people.

CHAPTER 21

Arrival in Greece

Athens

June 1993

Athens airport is rundown and chaotic. It is the first test for my Greek language skills. I laboriously spell out Greek words.

'Exit, Customs...'

I am anxious as the others are relying on me to get us through.

My heart is beating fast, sweat beads appear on my forehead.

It is summer and very hot, even inside the airport building.

People crowd around us and push and shove. We are jet lagged and bewildered. My brain fuzzy. Have difficulty in doing anything.

"Are we in Athens yet?" asked Mother.

"Almost; have to go through customs first."

In one customs queue, people are hustled through customs. The customs officers do not check any passports, documents, or bags. A bored custom officer motions people through.

"Hurry up, move on," he said.

We queue in this line, and he waves us through.

I notice in the other queue, the customs officer reads documents, makes people open handbags, and quizzes them on their travel intentions.

It is bedlam; masses of people mill around trying to locate their bags and belongings. I stay with Mother who is swaying from jet lag and tiredness. The crowd moulds into a tight pack, Alan elbows his way into the scrum and retrieves our suitcases. Everyone has the tortured expression of long-distance travel.

Poor Mum looks lost, shaky.

"I would like to sleep," she said softly.

"I need to organise a taxi to the hotel and then you can sleep," I said.

Have I done the right thing taking Mother to Greece? Maybe Jim was right.

Mother is spacey from sleep deprivation and clings to me. Alan struggles with all our suitcases.

Somehow my Greek is good enough to be understood to hire a taxi.

The early morning drive through the mayhem of Athens streets frights me; every so often the traffic snarls and blocks. The taxi driver drops us off at the Stanley Hotel at 5 a.m. However, the hotel refuses us access to our rooms until 7 a.m. Apparently, it is not policy to let people in early or they must pay double. We cool our cranky, tired heels dozing in a corner of the foyer until seven. Mother looks unwell.

The view of the street from the hotel is

depressing—derelict buildings, smog, intense traffic, thick pollution. This is not what I expected.

Eventually, at seven, we are given the room keys and allowed into our rooms. We throw the bags to the floor and crash until midday. Shower, eat a light lunch of thin slices of veal and roast potato. Mother is refreshed and talkative; she has made a super effort to keep up. I am very proud of her.

"Can we visit the Acropolis?" Mother said. "The last time I saw the Acropolis was in 1952 when we left Greece."

At the Acropolis, Mother loses momentum trying to climb the steep steps. So, Mother and I stay on the wooden bench and drink a cold frappe. It is scorching hot. Perspiration runs down our noses. Alan organises himself a quick tour of the main parts of the Acropolis with an English guide.

We abandon the shopping trip. Mother is too tired to think or speak. Return to the Stanley Hotel, put her to bed. She falls asleep immediately. Alan and I share a cold beer and practise my fractured Greek with the locals.

Later Alan and I catch the lift to the roof garden. Athens is transformed several stories up, it is nothing like the street view. All residential buildings around the Acropolis must be a certain height not to block the view, no high-rise monstrosities. The view is stunning, we stare in awe at the Acropolis. It is magnificent, bathed in coloured red and blue lights and sits on a hill 156 metres high. Apparently built by Pericles in the fifth century BC as a monument to the achievements of the inhabitants of Athens. It stands connecting the ancient past to the present. The hill is rocky and steep on all sides except for the western side and the splendour of this building is breathtaking. I recall the cult of Athena, the city's patron goddess.

Back in our room, I dream of Athena the goddess.

CHAPTER 22

Coming home

Mytilene

June 1993

Mother lights a candle at the small white church at the airport when we land at Mytilene. We endure a slow drive to the hotel, stare unbelieving at the surroundings. The town is a picture postcard of what a Greek island should be; grape vines hanging over shops and houses. A picturesque port with small fishing vessels and larger palatial boats which ooze wealth. Motorbikes roar by; no one wears a helmet. Young men and women hang on tight on motorbikes and scooters. The noise deafening.

We check into the Blue Seas Hotel in the late afternoon. It is very clean and simple; our rooms overlook the port. The hotel has sixty-one furnished rooms, and each room with its own veranda and magnificent view.

'Here, time is converted to a fourth dimension,' said the blurb on the hotel brochure.

I read that Mytilene, the capital, has been an organised city since 1054 BC according to the writings of Homer. Aristotle lived on Mytilene for two years, 337-335 BC. History and religion are important to the island. The ninth century Byzantine saints; Saint George the Archbishop of Mytilene, Saint Symeon of Lesvos, and Saint David the Monk.

Mytilene's port has many ferries to the nearby islands of Lemnos and Chios and Ayvalik in Turkey. The island produces ouzo, exports sardines, olives, and woodwork. The town is built on seven hills.

In the short time since our arrival, Mother has morphed into a different person and cheerfully natters in Greek to total strangers, something she would never do in Melbourne.

~

Yesterday, as we waited for the connecting flight from Athens to Mytilene, the announcer said in Greek "Go to Gate Seven for the plane to Mytilene."

Mother jumped up and shouted, "Come on, let's go," as she darted in the direction of Gate Seven.

Alan and I looked at each other; it was the first sign of energy I had seen in her for ages.

~

Here in Mytilene, the atmosphere is electric; we are gapemouthed as we wander the sleepy streets. Houses with masses of creepers with bright purple and red flowers. I can barely contain myself with excitement and ask direction of an old man. Mother butts in.

"Do you know Renulla Mater?" she asked.

"No," he said.

Mother looked disappointed.

She directs us up and down streets. Normally hesitant and half-blind with glaucoma, here she sees and follows a clear map in her memory.

"Look," she said pointing in the distance, "St Theodore Church; I must light a candle there tomorrow."

"This is the house where my cousin used to live," she said touching the fence, a small smile on her face.

"Your Father and I visited her before she died."

We stop at a tall green fence.

"Your brothers attended this school." She said, a wide beam of light on her face.

As if on cue, a soccer ball bounces over the fence and falls near us from the primary school at our feet. Two boys rush out of the green gate and retrieve the ball.

The shady trees are cool in the sticky heat. Everywhere we go brings shouts of pleasure from Mother. She is reliving a previous life. We are anchored to her recollections.

I have never seen her so energetic.

A delicious food aroma drifts in the air, the tantalising smell of roast lamb. We locate the open-air restaurant and order. The food delicious, we eat with vigour and appreciation.

"This is the best lamb I have tasted," said Alan.

We mop the last morsels on the plates with thick bread. Two small cats nibble on tiny bits of lamb that I drop on the ground for them. At some stage, I forget to feed them and they gently mew at me for more.

A deaf girl stops at our table and shows us a note in Greek asking for money. I give her some. Watch a group of gypsy women go past.

Mother is animated, her voice loud and excited, rising in pitch. The life she used to have has come back to her.

I am exhausted and my feet hurt. But Mother is a ball of energy.

"Thank you so much for bringing me home to Mytilene; thank you, thank you," she said.

"This is a dream come true for me. I never thought I would see my island again."

She kisses us both, hugs us tight, tears run down her face. Alan and I have moist eyes. We see Mytilene with tourist eyes; the small local shops, the well-preserved white painted houses, bright red plants hanging in pots from balconies. But Mother is experiencing Mytilene from her heart; from deep memories, long-lost people, and remembered events.

CHAPTER 23

Exploring the old world

Mytilene

June 1993

"I want to visit the old cemetery today," Mother said.

"Why?" I asked, baffled as it seems such a strange request. "Who is buried there?"

"No one you know," she said.

I raise my eyebrows and say nothing. Much of the time I am in the dark as to her rationale for going to places. She still sees me as a child. Her manner mysterious. There is a movie screen inside her head that is replaying the past. She holds deep secrets. I accept that but wish I knew more.

The small cemetery is tucked away in a heavily wooded area, has burial plots surrounded with iron and plaques. Is green and peaceful; creepers and flowers grow wild over graves and up the sides of trees. The small white-washed church has a metal cross on the roof. There is a larger building next to the church. The interior of the shed-like building is dark and gloomy, has a creepy atmosphere. My hairs stand on end. When my eyes adjust to the dark, I can see shelves and shelves of wooden boxes, apparently holding dead people's bones.

"Space is limited here," said the black moustached keeper of the shed.

"At a certain date, each grave is dug up, the bones cleaned, and the bones packed in the boxes you see," he waved his hands to the direction of the boxes.

"They are marked by name and year; families can still come and respect their dead many years after they die."

Mother nods in agreement. Alan pulls a face and shrugs his shoulders when I translate what the man has said.

"Seems a bit creepy," he said.

We spent some time at the discrete white church. It has the usual icons and flickering candles. Funeral services are held here. Mother did not give me any more information as to why this church was meaningful to her past. I do learn it is customary to donate money to the priest.

"Who would you like me to pray for?" said the priest. He has a solemn face, held out his hand out to receive the money.

I wrote 'Michael Evangelou' on a scrap of paper, the priest placed the note in his pocket, with the money.

Would Father have been pleased we have returned to Mytilene?

Mother lights several candles, crosses herself,

kisses every icon she can reach. I light a candle and don't do much kissing. Alan watches, this is very strange to him.

As we step outside the cemetery, I notice an elderly man leading a brown donkey. Two large, metal canisters of milk are attached to the sides of the animal. The man delivers milk to homes, as he has done for years. He scoops the milk from the canister into the waiting milk jugs the women provide. The man is short has an impressive black moustache. His baggy pants held by a rope around his waist.

"Can I take your photo?" I said.

He nods and rubs the donkey's ears, grooming him for the photo. Smiles, appears eager to have his photo taken standing next to the donkey.

"I want to see our old home in Thyra Street," said Mother.

"We need to ask directions to the old house as I don't remember the way to Thyra Street," she said.

I ask directions of a slim, dark-haired woman holding the hand of a curly-haired little girl.

"Where are you from?" the woman said.

When I tell her, she turns to the girl.

"These people are from Australia. The land of jumping kangaroos."

The girl laughs.

"She has a toy kangaroo at home," said the woman.

"My Mother wants to see her old home in Thyra Street. Can you help us?" I said.

"I can take you there as it is a little difficult as the road has changed," the woman said.

She walks with us to Thyra Street; Mother kept asking about people I had never heard of.

"Here it is, straight up, the street is very steep, tell your Mother to be careful. Good luck; hope you find what you are looking for." She said.

Thyra Street is steep, I hold Mother's arm tightly, she is unsteady. The cobblestones are slippery.

We pass old two-storey houses tightly squashed on both sides of the cobbled road. Young boys chase each other in front of us. They stop when we go past, know we are strangers to the area, and curious as to where we are going.

"Here it is," Mother said, her voice a shout.

"I scrubbed those tiles on my hands and knees a thousand times," she said, pointing to a house ahead of us. Her voice is light and happy.

"How could I forget them?"

And she was right. It was the house, checked the address against my notes.

Mother is flushed with expectation. We three stand at the front door, the small boys who now shadowing us.

I knock on the door, am nervous as what to say. I am a stranger with poor language skills meeting another stranger about a house. Mother next to me. Alan at the back. My heart beats fast. This is all new to me.

A soft-faced, older woman in her sixties opens the door.

"Excuse me," I said in Greek, "this used to be our family's home...." Before I can finish my sentence, Mother runs up to her.

"It is me, Ekaterini Evangelou, we sold you this house," she said.

The woman at the door recognises Mother, hugs her. The two women speak in excited Greek. They talk so fast I have trouble keeping up with the conversation.

"I want to show you around the house. Can you come back on Monday?" The woman said.

We agree, although I can see Mother was disappointed; she wanted to see inside the house now. Perhaps the house was messy, and the woman wanted to tidy up so it would look good for Mother's inspection. The soft-faced woman has lived in this house with her husband for more than forty-one years. The daughter married and has her own home nearby.

Mother is elated, almost dancing with pleasure. Locating the old home is a real coup for her. She gossips about this neighbour and that as we creep carefully down the steep hill. Mother hangs onto me tightly. Alan trails behind.

It is steaming hot, we sweat and decide to return

to the hotel and rest. I locate a laundry nearby and organise our washing.

In the afternoon, Mother said, "Can we look for your Father's sister Harikula's house?"

I have the envelope with the address on the back. Again, we are detectives searching for clues for the street.

"Did you find the house?"

I turn around; it is the same long-haired woman with the child who I asked directions previously.

"You are close to Saphous Street," she said and gestures in the direction.

Mother's memory kicks in and like a homing pigeon; she takes us to the Harikula house.

Again, nervously knocks on the door. A gentle-faced, middle-aged woman opens the door.

"We are from Australia. I am the daughter of Ekaterini Evangelou," I point to Mother. "Mother is the wife of Michael Evangelou; I understand you are related to my Father."

I hold my breath. Was I understood? What if it is the wrong house? What if the people had moved and now belonged to another family?

There is silence. The woman gazes at Mother for a few moments for the statement to sink in.

"Thea Ekaterini," (Aunt Katherine) said the woman. She puts her arms out, holds Mother tightly for a long time. Mother pats her back.

It feels surreal, as though Mother had been to

the shops and returned and not been away for forty-one years since she has been here.

The woman's name is Renulla, the daughter of Father's sister Harikula, who is dead.

"Such a story I have to tell you, Renulla," Mother said and beams.

Alan stands open-mouthed. I grin.

"Come in, come in," said Renulla, grabs Mother's hand. Alan and I follow.

Renulla's home is spotless, everything in its place. The walls are white and appear to be freshly painted. The home has small ornaments and bric-a-brac on embroidered cloths. Black-and-white photos of old men with moustaches and wedding groups in wooden frames hold pride of place on the walls. Lacy curtains flap in the breeze. It is deliciously cool inside after the tormenting heat outside.

"Sit down," said Renulla patting the divan. She turns to a man already sitting on the divan.

"This is Taci," she said.

Mother recognises him. He is the son of another of Father's brothers, visiting from Athens.

Renulla is an engaging, gentle woman with soft, twinkling brown eyes. She moves effortlessly around her home and places plates of crystallised grapefruit with glasses of cold water in front of us.

"Eat," she said.

"I will make coffee soon."

"Don't you remember me?" Taci said to me. "You wrote to me in English when you were a young girl with pigtails. I was stationed in Germany at the time, serving as part of the combined world peace mission after the war."

An image came to my mind. I had come across the letters from Taci before we left. Read them with interest. It seemed another lifetime ago. Father had died. Mother thought it a good idea for me to write to Taci. And am amazed that Taci would remember my childish writings.

Am flushed, mute, listen, watch, take in the hum of conversations. It feels like a movie, relatives from the past, still connected to us, still alive.

"Where are you staying? How long will you be here?" Said Taci.

There is no way I could have predicted the amazing few days in Mytilene. I feel as though I am awake in a dream. But it is real. These people are my family and I am a part of them.

The door opens and Renulla's husband Michael arrives, again shouts of pleasure and embraces.

Alan tries to get a word in, everyone speaks to him in Greek. I translate back and forth. Mother does not stop talking, making up for forty-one years' gossip.

"What happened to my cousin?" She said.

"Where is the sister of the uncle?" Her questions spill out.

She is special to these people. They have a history with Mother that I can only guess at, shared experiences, shared stories. I understood what she has lost all those years leaving these lovely people behind in Lesvos. Mother never wanted to leave. It was Father's dream to relocate to Australia, but it ended in tragedy. Father died, no money, three kids, and no way to return. Mother was stuck in a country she never wanted to be in.

Later we stroll along the harbour, locate a small restaurant with a clear view of the sea. Share a meal of delicious stuffed peppers, grilled eggplant, roast potatoes, and tomatoes. The food melts in our mouths, the salad fresh. Excited conversations, questions and answers overlap. We promise to meet again soon.

Mother cannot stop laughing.

She calls me her pet name, "Calel."

CHAPTER 24

Relatives

Mytilene

June 1993

From the balcony of the Blue Sea Hotel, the sea shimmers in the blackness. Blurred lights are reflected from nearby houses and shapes of buildings reflect in the inky water. Small fishing boats drift off to sea. It is 11 p.m. and still warm. The sky is dark except for one lone shining star. The houses on the hill are ablaze with miniscule lights. They have become beacons showing a path up the mountain.

Below, Mytilene pulsates with people and cars. Couples walk with arms around each other. Assorted families and singles promenade along the harbour and populate the bustling noisy restaurants. Bouzouki music filters out. The relentless traffic moans and groans with motorbikes, scooters, and cars.

How can an island sustain so many vehicles?

The Greek navy ships that were in the port yesterday are out on patrol somewhere. The navy is commonly around Lesvos and especially Mytilene. It is deemed a conflict zone for the Greeks due to the proximity of Lesvos to the Turkish mainland. There has been a long and sordid history of centuries of hatred and bloody wars between the two countries.

Alan is unwell and feverish. He has come down with the flu. I provide Panadol, vitamin C drinks, and sympathy.

Mother is fine, hard to get going in the mornings when she is distant and distracted. Breakfast is in the dining room of the Blue Sea Hotel. Always the same: a buffet with choices of cake, boiled eggs, cruskets, cold meat, cheese, and coffee. After eating, Mother is brighter, laughs, engages with the world. It is a marvel to see my normally downcast Mother so happy.

"Good morning," Mother said to a staff member at breakfast.

"How did you sleep?"

"How is your trip going?" said the waitress.

"Have you caught up on any relatives?"

With that Mother launches into the story of meeting up with Renulla and Taci.

Am kept busy all day being her personal nurse and guide. Wake her up, toilet, shower, dress, give medicines, eye drops. Put her to bed. I am her eyes and ears. Point out things of interest. Mother has not said, "I cannot see" as she normally does.

Mother sleeps in the adjunct room next to ours at the hotel. Alan and I need time together. She needs a break from us also. It has worked so far.

Must remember to encourage her to have a longer rest in the afternoon.

~

Today has been another remarkable day. It is hard to know where it starts and ends. It has been a kaleidoscope of activity and magic. Want to write it down and remember everything. I am still nervous speaking in Greek; some words are unknown to me. A few conversations leave me behind as I try to grasp for the correct Greek word. People are kind and patient to my fumbled attempts.

~

Earlier in the day, Taci arrived at our hotel in a taxi.

"I am your tour guide today," he said bowing. "My mission is to show you the sights of Lesvos."

This is unexpected, a surprise. We squeeze into the taxi.

The taxi driver points out things of interest as we drive along. I translate everything to Alan; Mother smiles and is content.

Every so many kilometres, on the side of the road are small white boxes on the ground. They are marked with crosses and photos of dead people. These are the spots where people have crashed their cars or motorcycles and died. I counted more than forty of these boxes in a short time before I stopped counting.

The lack of helmets for scooter drivers and motorbikes worries me.

Girls ride on scooters with long hair streaming out like goddesses. Whole families ride pillion clinging to each other.

The roads are dangerous and often narrow. I can't get used to the cars driving on the opposite side of the road to Australia. Even crossing the road as a pedestrian is an art, as you don't know where to watch for cars.

Taci is urbane, a mixture of generosity and sadness.

"My wife died three years ago," said Taci.

"I miss her very much. I often stay at Renulla's and Michael's for company." He looks forlorn.

"I have a son, but he is in the army. And a daughter I do not see as we argue all the time." He looks out of the car window.

"My brother Panayiotis and his family live in the apartment one floor underneath my Athens apartment."

Taci is about fifty to fifty-five, steely white hair, handsome as older Greek men are. He is a solicitor. Understands English but speaks Greek to Alan and I translate. Maybe he is as I am, unsure of the words. Is respectful towards Mother and chooses places to visit with the understanding of the oldies and their obsession with religion and churches. Mother loves the churches and monasteries, lights candles. Kisses icons; feels blessed.

Taci leans over and says in a quiet voice only I can hear.

"One day, I will tell you the reason why your father left Lesvos." He glances at Mother who is peering out of the window.

"Not today, I don't want to upset your Mother."

It piques my interest, something about Father's brothers—a feud perhaps? Did my parents leave Lesvos because of some family issue? It is news to me. No one has spoken of this to me before, certainly not Mother. Am unsure about stirring old problems and anxieties. But want to know more.

"Your father was a wonderful man, highly principled and intelligent," Taci said in a loud voice.

Mother nods in agreement.

"Sadly, my own Father had none of the good qualities your Father had..." he said, his voice cracked and stopped speaking.

When we were at Renulla's house yesterday, her husband Michael referred to my Father with great affection. Father was the youngest in the family of four brothers and one sister. Renulla said Father was the most caring towards his Mother and Father especially as they aged and became ill. He would pop in after work and see if his parents needed any shopping or assistance with anything. The other brothers were too busy with their business interests to spend time with the parents.

Why did Father leave Mytilene to come to Australia, to lose so much and against the wishes of

Mother? Most migrants leave for a better life. Father left for a much poorer life. There is so much I do not know.

Alan talks to Taci, asks questions about the island, I translate his words back and forth.

Alan is the odd man out, he has never known what it is like to have poor language skills and struggle to be understood.

We visit Agios Raphael and Abbey Ermogenis and monastery. We are told Agios Raphael has been worshipped as a saint and believed to have worked miracles. The present buildings host pilgrims in guesthouses. The public can apply to stay for the weekend in the plain rooms with only a bed, for meditation and rest. Quite impressive, it has an underground grotto and underground well, several ancient paintings of historical relevance, and many religious sculptures.

The taxi takes us to a church famous for the Archangel Michael Taxiarchis at Mantamados. Legend says that the monastery was attacked by Turks who slaughtered the monks except for one who managed to crawl up on the roof. When it was over, the monk took clay and mixed it with the blood of his fellow monks who were killed and made an icon, in which the archangel is black. The place has a peculiar atmosphere; it reeks of old. I half expect a ghost to appear before me, at least to slip through closed doors. Hundreds of candles flicker, suddenly the flames lean to one direction as though unseen movement has disturbed them. Then they settle.

"This is wonderful," said Mother.

She is in her element, bowing, crossing herself, lighting candles.

"What is this all about?" said Alan bewildered by the religiosity of the island and people. He follows no religion.

"Make sure you pay the priest to pray for your Father," Mother said.

The grey-haired priest writes 'Michael Evangelou' on a long list of prayer requests and pops it and the money in his pocket.

About twenty-seven km from Mytilene is Ayiassos village built on the slopes of Mount Olymbos. I am told that over the years, the village has taken the role of the guardian of Orthodox faith. The stone-paved streets and traditional tile-roofed houses are ancient. Nearby are dense forests of chestnut and pine trees. The church Panayia tis Ayiasiotissa is the dominant feature of the village. It is as if we stepped back to the seventeenth century or earlier. The village in a time warp, with stone-paved streets, traditional tile-roofed stone houses and hanging vines of masses of purple wisteria flowers. I am captivated, enthralled.

The people in this area know Australia well. Many migrated to Australia for a better life, made their fortune and returned home with the spoils to live with family. Others came back poorer than before.

"Are you from Australia?" said one shopkeeper in Greek.

"Yes," I said.

"Where do you live?" he said.

"Melbourne," I said.

"My son lived in Preston in Melbourne for ten years. He has returned home with a wife and children and opened a shop in Mytilene." He said.

"How are you going, mate?" He said, in an exaggerated Australian accent.

"Or right, mate," I said.

We laugh.

At the highest part of the steep slopes of Ayiassos village, you can see the continent of Turkey, as it looks mournfully out to sea. It intrigues me. Taci and Mother tell harrowing stories about bloody wars with the Turks, conflict seeped in centuries of fighting.

Lunch is at a delightful restaurant called Small Madonna, right on the sand a few footsteps from the sea. There is no menu, only the catch of the day. We share delicious crisp fried fish, roasted potatoes, fresh salad with chunks of feta cheese. This is followed by baklava and coffee. My sense of taste, smell, hearing, sight, and touch are aroused by the sea and the aroma from the food and cheerful conversations. It is an enchanted meal.

Taci refuses to let me pay for anything, although I offer many times.

He teases me as though I am his little sister. He possesses a sharp mind, is energetic, and never stops smoking. There are no rules about smoking in Lesvos; everyone seems to smoke everywhere.

Taci tells me the last time my family and his met was in 1952. Our family stayed with Taci's family in Athens for a few days before we migrated to Australia. I was a child of four, I remember my brothers John and Jim, and Taci and his brother tormenting me. They jumped out from behind a door wearing gas masks left over from the war. I ran away screaming.

Mother beams with pleasure, reminisces about the past.

Alan's flu has not slowed him down. He asks questions and takes an interest in everything.

I pinch myself to see if I am awake.

The taxi driver returns us to The Blue Sea Hotel in the evening.

"Thank you, Taci for a magnificent day," I said and meant it.

"We are indebted to you," said Mother, holding Taci's hand.

"Thank you, it has been a very interesting day," said Alan.

"Nonsense, it's my pleasure," Taci said and drives away with the taxi driver.

Mother and I ride the creaky, two-person lift to our floor. Snuggle her in her bed, she falls asleep before I close the door behind me. Alan is already asleep in our room.

I cannot rest. I am wide awake and jot the day's activities in my journal.

In the evening, I venture out alone to purchase take-away food from one of the many restaurants nearby. Mother and Alan are both too tired to go out for a meal. I wander around the restaurants at 10:30 p.m. and feel safe. Tourist shops are still open. Many people are out eating and drinking, walking and talking. Decide on the restaurant we used before; the owner recognises me and packages a variety of delicious meat and vegetables in foil.

On my return to the hotel, I wake Mother and Alan. We eat in our room. Mother, Alan and I devour the lot.

A surprising aspect of this trip is that I am developing an image of myself as a person with a Greek heritage and Greek ancestry and family.

I wonder what Mytilene it is like in winter. They tell me it snows sometimes.

CHAPTER 25

The castle

Mytilene

June 1993

I relish the early morning peacefulness of the small white balcony at The Blue Sea Hotel. The comings and goings of the harbour, boats, oil tankers, navy ships are familiar to me now. All life in Mytilene centres on the harbour. Police drive up to the harbour as another cruise ship arrives. The air has a hazed gold; it promises to be another hot day. A dog barks in the background. Cars, motorbikes, and Vespas race past, continue their relentless pursuit of roads and places to go. By 6:20 a.m., most of the parking spots around the harbour are taken. I watch a huge oil tanker dock in the harbour. Loud, male Greek voices reverberate from microphones. Taxis scream past. A sailor in uniform closes a gate near departures.

Starlings are fearless and dance on the balcony next to me. They make their nests over the external lights, must be uncomfortable when the lights are switched on.

I wonder how my children are in Australia. I

miss them. It would be wonderful to share this Greek adventure with them. They could meet the delightful people that are their relatives.

I am amazed at Mother with her many physical and mental problems; she is another person here. I am finding pieces of Mother here in Mytilene, the pieces that were hidden or thrown away when she left the island.

~

Yesterday, in the early cool morning, while Mother slept, Alan and I strolled to the old Castle. I have read much about the Castle, it dates back for centuries. Its foundations laid by Justinian the Byzantine Emperor in the fifth century BC, then fortified by Genoese and Venetians. During summer, the Castle is used for performances by musicians, operas, and other musical and artistic events. We passed the enormous pine tree forest that stretches from the Castle to the beach. But we couldn't have access to the Castle grounds as they were locked. A young soldier stood guard outside, on overnight point duty. We later come across him drinking coffee with his friends at an outdoor café.

"I remember you were the soldier on point duty," I said.

He smiled and said, "Yes."

Alan and I explore the area, find the rocky beach, and return to the hotel.

Wake Mother and get her ready, have our usual breakfast.

~

Mother has plans to pray at Saint Theodore's church today. His petrified remains are kept at this church. I have read many references made about the miracles attributed to this saint. In 1832, when Lesvos was controlled by Turkey, a devastating plague hit the population of Mytilene and many died. Residents were forced to abandon their homes and flee to the hills. Doctors from Constantinople and medicines were dispatched but nothing helped. Saint Theodore appeared in a dream to Father Kallinikos, and he urged the people to gather from the mountains and pray. The body of Saint Theodore was exhumed, and his bones carried in a box. Father Kallinikos ordered the bones to be carried in a procession around the church. From that moment, no one died from the plague, neither Christian nor Turk. Each year, a feast day is established, and thousands of people watch the procession of the remains of Saint Theodore through the town.

Mother tells a story of the spirit of Saint Theodore and how he aided a ship captain to avoid Italian gunfire during World War II.

"Saint Theodore stood next to the captain and guided him to steer his ship in a zig-zag fashion." She moves her hands back and forth.

"The captain was saved and none of the Italian bombs hit his boat," she said.

We light candles for Saint Theodore and the dead.

Mytilene has many religious connections. The Apostle Paul landed in Mytilene in 52 A.D. on his way to Chios.

I wonder what Mother is thinking these days? She has always been a closed book, has another deep life, no one can reach. There is a part of her that frightens me, the part that hears voices and is terrified by them. So far on this trip, I have not heard much of the voices. Although does she mutter to herself and pick her lips. My impression is that she is enjoying the trip.

~

Today, outside Saint Theodore's church, I notice a gypsy woman dressed in a gaily coloured dress and head scarf, cradling a 'sick child.' She holds out an outstretched hand for money. Of course, I hand her money. Later in the day, notice the gypsy woman and her sick child playing catch with a ball.

The gypsies have a good thing going, hanging around the churches. People who have crossed themselves a few thousand times and have lit several candles are ripe for compassionate giving.

Mother and I meander around the old marketplace in Ermou Street. Men and women carry laden string bags purchased from the family-run shops selling food, clothes, shoes and tourist paraphilia, postcards and souvenirs. Shopkeepers greet the shoppers by name; everyone seems to know each other. The cobblestone street is closed to traffic during the time the stores are open. We peer into shops, take in the bustling atmosphere. Along the way meet an elderly man the same age as Mother; they attended school together and knew each other in Mytilene. He is married to a cousin of a cousin of Mother's. He still owns a butcher's shop in Ermou Street and often works there. They recognise each other and have a lively conversation about mutual friends and acquaintances.

Mother directs us to the old café her Father once ran. It is now boarded up. She tells stories about the times she helped run coffee to the customers when she was a girl.

"I loved helping my Father," she said.

"He and I were very close. Much closer than my Mother." Her face crumpled, I thought she was going to cry.

"Bless his soul," she said and crossed herself. "Bless his wonderful soul."

We return to the hotel, Mother takes a nap. The trek back to the hotel is long and tiring. The blazing sunshine makes for weariness.

While she sleeps, Alan and I return to the Castle. The gates are open, we explore the grounds and buildings. The old buildings are in various stages of decay, contain deep secret tunnels, and were used as shelters for women and children during battles with the Turks. The tunnels were designed with openings that allowed light and air and extend under the town into secret exits.

One side of the Castle is a fortress looking out to the sea, still standing guard in case of an invasion from Turkey. I am told that the castle had been formally mentioned in documents as early as 1260 and renovated in 1373. Some parts reflect the Turkish occupation. The castle has three main building stages: Byzantine, Genoese, and Turkish. It was one of the stronger castles and thought impossible to conquer at one stage.

It is scorching, red-faced hot; we stop periodically to drink water and get our breath.

A carpet of wild red and white poppies and small yellow flowers cover the ground of the castle. Tourists from the cruise ship that is moored in the harbour stroll around the castle grounds. They appear to be English tourists, easily identified with their wide hats and white legs.

We return to the hotel and collect Mother. Lunch at an open-air restaurant near the harbour. The man who owns the place knows us now and we are greeted with affection. We are pointed to the best table in the restaurant which has a magnificent view of the blue harbour. Order a delicious veal casserole, the meat tender, the vegetables perfect.

Back at The Blue Sea, there is a message from Renulla asking us to meet at her house at 5 p.m.

At five o'clock, we move slowly to Renulla's house. Mother is awkward and hangs on to to me.

At Renulla's, we are shepherded into the cool courtyard. Masses of green vines spill languidly from the veranda. Bright red geraniums in square tins surround the small courtyard.

The conversations and questions and answers continue thick and fast. We sip cold lemonade and nibble on olives and cheese.

"Do you have any photos of Mother and Father when they were younger?" I asked.

Renulla grins. Disappears and returns with a wide cardboard box filled to the brim with black-and-white photos. Stories spill out with the photos. It is a magical box, the past locked inside.

"This is your Father when he became engaged to your Mother," she says, placing the photos on the table like a piece of a jigsaw puzzle.

I peer at the photo; this is Father young with thick wavy hair and handsome, Mother holds a shy smile, long hair, and perfect features.

As though reading my mind, Renulla said, "Your mother was quite a catch for your father. There were others who wanted to marry her, but she chose your Father."

Mother blushed.

"This is your grandfather and grandmother," said Renulla.

A grey-haired elderly man and woman hold two squirming boys. They are my brothers John and

Jim. There is only eighteen months between them; they were both toddlers. I carry the name of the grandmother in the photo, Calliope. Michael, the grandfather, has his name passed on to each family, including my Father. It is a Greek custom to name one child after your parents.

"This is your father and mother at your christening," Renulla said.

The photo shows a beautiful, smiling young woman with short dark hair, holding a small baby. The baby is me. Father looks proud in the photo, two godparents next to him. My brothers are seated in the background, surrounded by smiling men and woman and children. These are my relatives, aunts, uncles, cousins, my family.

Peer closely at the photos, reflecting on a life that I have no recollection.

One of Renulla's sons, Nicholas, and his wife Narcia join us with their two children. It has become a party.

Taci is in fine form, telling jokes; I translate them for Alan.

The photos have triggered memories in Mother. She shares stories of family picnics with cousins in the forest. As if on cue, Renulla lays another part of the jigsaw on the table. A photo of a group of happy men and women and children enjoying a picnic in a pine forest. I am a baby of about eighteen months, sitting on a large, checked blanket on the ground; next to me a large watermelon the same size as me.

The doorbell rings; a neighbour is invited to join us.

"You have to shout in her left ear as she is very deaf," said Renulla, pointing to her ears.

"She swims in the sea each day to keep fit."

I am impressed; the woman is older than Mother.

Taci suggests Alan and I go with him to have an ouzo. Mother frowns; is annoyed I am going without her. We walk to the farthest part of the harbour, where a fisherman's café is hidden from view. The café is in the middle of the harbour connected by a narrow causeway, is an ouzeria. We are served ouzo and mezedes, feta cheese, tomatoes and olives. We observe the ships leaving for Athens and the ferry returning from Turkey. The café is full of old fishermen drinking coffee and ouzo, watching the lights of the city as darkness falls.

"This café is not for the posh," said Taci, a grin on his face.

"Why did my Father leave Lesvos?" I asked.

"It is a complicated story. I did not want to discuss it in front of your Mother as I have no wish to upset her." Taci downs a glass of ouzo and orders another.

"Your father had financial problems, something to do with investing in grain, but the venture failed, and he was out of pocket by a large amount of money."

I sip my ouzo, translate for Alan.

"Your Father asked his brothers for assistance,

but they turned their backs on him and did not support him. I understand he lost a lot of money and had to sell your home and had no other choice but to emigrate," Taci said.

I am shocked.

"Your Father's brothers could have helped him, but they did not. Even my own Father who was wealthy, refused," he said.

We sip our drinks, two weather-beaten old men near us laugh uproariously.

"Things did not get better in Australia," I said.

"Father's accountancy qualifications were not recognised in Australia. The only work he could find was in a terrible factory at Fishermen's Bend. He was ill-equipped to work with his hands, as he always used his brains. He was injured at work; his hand needed an operation." I said.

I glance at the ferry coming closer to the harbour. This is hard for me.

"My parents struggled to make ends meet; we were poor. Father grew our food and we had chickens for eggs mother cooked and made all our clothes."

I swallow hard. It still brings strong emotions in me.

"In 1956, Father was killed by a drunk driver. He had no life insurance." I stop.

"We had no money for a funeral. Neighbours held a collection for us that enabled us to pay for the funeral and bury Father." I turn my head away.

"It was an immense tragedy for Mother with three children to feed and clothe and educate."

There are tears in Taci's eyes and he reaches for his handkerchief.

"My brothers had to leave high school to support us financially." I couldn't go on any further.

"There is so much sadness in both my parents' families. Mother left for Australia on bad terms with her Mother because Father had to sell the Thyra street house. Her brother Yannis and her Mother had planned to live in the Thyra House," I said.

"They were angry with father, refused to see the family off."

The moon is a bright, round ball over the dark sea.

We sit in comfortable silence and nibble on olives and tomatoes.

"My father tried to seduce my wife. He was a wicked man," Taci said suddenly.

Shocked, unsure what to say to that. Nod and listen.

"My wife died of cancer despite the best medical treatment and expert doctors. I miss her so much," Taci looks thoughtful.

The sea beckons in the distance.

"My daughter will not speak to me. She is upset that I am now dating a twenty-eight-year-old model," he said.

I try not to show any reaction. Nod encouragingly. What can I say after that statement?

Taci passes a photo of his girlfriend. She is a long-legged brunette with round brown eyes and high cheekbones; she is of exceptional beauty.

"I was so lonely for female company after my wife died; my daughter did not understand. I dated a few women, but this girl loves me and has helped me overcome my grief."

He refills his ouzo, pops a black olive in his mouth and picks at the feta cheese.

"Renulla and Michael threw me out of their house when they heard about my relationship with the girl. She is my daughter's age."

He signals the waiter. "But I have made up with Renulla and Michael."

"I bought a house in Mytilene; when it is renovated I hope to introduce my girlfriend to the relatives. She is in Athens now, on a fashion shoot."

Taci's stories are complex and need time to process.

"We better go back," I said. "Mother will be worried."

On our way back, we come across Renulla's husband Michael drinking with his friends in another café. He jumps up, looks embarrassed. Perhaps Renulla asked him to be home to be with us.

"Michael likes to drink," said Taci in a whisper.

We pass a communist party rally assembling in the square, a mass of rowdy, shouting people, loud beating drums, and trumpets.

Mother corners me when we return to Renulla's house. "Where have you been?" Mother said.

"We had ouzo with Taci," I said.

"What did you talk about?" she said, eyes narrow.

"He said he bought a house in Mytilene that he is renovating," I said.

"Would you all like to stay here at my house? You will be made very welcome," said Renulla, her arms around Mother's waist as they move to the kitchen.

It sounds like a perfect idea but is problematic. Mother cannot climb the very steep stairs to the bedrooms in Renulla's house. After discussion, we resolve to continue at the Blue Seas Hotel; it has a lift.

"If you like, I can look after your Mother, and you and Alan might like to go out together for the day," Renulla said.

"That would be perfect," I said.

Later, back at the Hotel, help Mother to bed, she asks me more questions about our conversations with Taci.

"He has a girlfriend," I said. "He bought a house in Mytilene and is renovating it."

She looks at me with suspicion.

There is a message from Cousin Calliope, the daughter of another of Father's brothers. She wants us to be at her home on Tuesday at 7 p.m.

CHAPTER 26

Unanswered questions

Mytilene

June 1993

Today has been overwhelming. Tantalising secrets hinted at; things I did not know. It is like digging for treasure. There are bits of shining history being unearthed. Who knows what there is yet to be discovered.

Mother, Alan, and I hire a taxi, and return to the old home at Thyra Street. The lady who owns the house invited us back to inspect the old home. The woman, whose name I forgot, has a ready smile, could be any age. She cares for a husband who is bent over with arthritis and has dementia. The house has many steep places for the old man to fall. Perhaps he already tripped and hurt himself. Today he is wedged in a chair which is pushed tight next to a table. A wide cloth anchors him to the chair. He keeps trying to get up. It must be a full- time job keeping him safe.

The house is old, shabby, has major cracks on the walls in the kitchen and living areas. Needs to be repainted and has an ancient cooking range, however, the house is spotless.

The stairs to the bedrooms are almost vertical. I cling onto the balustrade for support and hold Mother as we work our way up the stairs. It is hard to believe once Mother ran up and down these stairs.

Mother cries out, "Come and see."

She points to a lamp in a corner of a small bedroom.

"Your father bought this lamp for you when you were a baby. You were afraid of the dark as a child."

I still am.

Every room brings another call from Mother.

"Look at this," she exclaims peering out of the green-shuttered window.

"I can see the neighbour's house. I used to wave to the neighbour like this," she leans out of the window and waves.

Mother is as excited as a child at her birthday party. I have an image in my mind of a youthful Mother putting the finishing touches to a meal, can see her wiping her hands on her apron as the door unlocks, calling to us children, "Father's home." And we race to greet him.

I have been told a story, when World War II ended there was a knock on the door. Mother opened the door to find a man with dirty, long hair and soiled ripped uniform standing at the entrance. Mother screamed and stepped back. She thought the man a vagrant.

"Don't you recognise your loving husband?" the man asked.

"It was only after I bathed him and cut his hair that I could embrace him as my husband," Mother said.

The story plays out in my mind. There is the front door, the bathroom here.

I try to reconnect to my personal memories of the house but can find nothing. I am governed by what I have been told by others. Have a sketch of the rooms of the house. Years ago, Mother mapped the house, every precise detail of rooms, windows, cupboards, and steps. When I compare her sketch to the actual house, everything is exactly as she remembered, etched perfectly in her mind.

I snap photo after photo. Listen to the conversations with the woman of the house and Mother. Alan tags behind us.

We check the backyard, again holding Mother's hand as she totters down the back steps.

She bursts into, "Look, look," and points to a huge, green clay container; it once held oil, now water.

"I remember you," she said to the container. Patting it like an old friend.

A wooden shed hides the outside toilet.

"In the winter time, going to the toilet was difficult as it was so cold," Mother said.

The small garden is lush, has purple wisteria growing over the fence, assorted colourful plants in olive oil tins. A clothesline with pegs anchored ready.

Mother's face is flushed, can barely breathe is so thrilled.

The aroma of coffee brings us back to the kitchen. We talk and nibble on freshly made baklava. The woman and Mother speak of the house as though speaking of a mutual friend.

"Do you have problems with the pipes in winter?" said Mother. "Does the kitchen pantry still squeak when you open it?"

The old man shouts and pushes at the table attempting to get up. The woman pats his hand, telling him she will take him for a walk soon. He settles with the sound of her voice. His hands shake, sips the coffee, shreds baklava into small pieces before placing them in his mouth.

At the end of our visit, Mother clasps the hands of the woman. "Thank you for looking after the old house so well."

The women embrace each other.

"Please come again," said the woman, the old man now by her side.

The narrow street fills with curious onlookers and small children. Word has gone out as to who we are. The street buzzes with noise. Mother is a star. Everyone wants to speak to her, shake her hand. Most of the neighbours still live here. We have been away more than forty years and the neighbours remember Mother as though she has been away for a short time.

One neighbour, who lives across the Thyra street house and not to be outdone, demands we visit her there and then. I try to explain about Mother's problem with stairs, but she will have none of our excuses. Demands we climb the steep spiral staircase on the outside of her house. It is very hard for Mother and she must stop many times to get her breath.

As soon as we were inside away from the prying eyes of the others in the street, she lets fly.

"I am so annoyed you left for Australia. Your son John has failed in his duties as a godfather to my son." She said.

This is a big sin in her eyes. Wonder if she is expecting money for compensation. She adds malicious words about my grandmother.

"Your father did not like your grandmother," she said pointing to me. "Ekaterina's mother was not welcome in the Thyra street house."

"Is this true?" I said.

Mother ignores me.

"Why have you not written?" the neighbour asks several times.

We eventually escape from the woman's clutches, pleading another appointment. Stumble down the stairs, onto the cobbled path to the market area.

Collect the photos that have been developed.

The owner notices me speaking to Alan in English.

"Are you Australians?" he asked. "I lived in Coburg for ten years," he said. "Has Collingwood won a premiership?"

We locate Renulla's husband's shop in the market. A line of customers wait to be served.

"Welcome, I have everything you need for nibbles. Cheese, bread, olives, salted sardines, smoked octopus," he said to the customers.

Sacks of rice, lentils, and dried broad beans bump into each other on the floor.

"Would you like to try my special cheese?" He asked us and cuts generous slices of his goat cheese.

"Best cheese ever," we said.

CHAPTER 27

Verga

June 1993

Am concerned the hectic pace of the last week may have a negative effect on Mother. Admittedly she has shown great stamina. But on occasions quite shaky, worn out. Last thing I need is to have her collapse and end up in hospital. Or, shudder, die.

It feels as if I am in a television series and the story is unfolding bit by bit. No central theme yet. No idea where the story will end or how.

Yesterday, again, the enigmatic Taci smiling broadly. He came with two taxis and Renulla and her husband. We divided up into two groups for each taxi for the day. Mother, Renulla, and I slip into one taxi. Taci, Michael, and Alan use the other taxi. The plan is to drive to the town of Verga in the mountains. This town has significance for Mother and her family. Her grandmother lived there, and she spent much time with her when she was young. Michael's sister lives in Verga, and we will be visiting her.

We pass thousands of green olive trees,

underneath the trees a carpet of yellow and white wild flowers. Lesvos is well known for its excellent olives and exports high-

quality olive oil. Some olive trees are hundreds of years old and with careful nurturing bear fruit each year. The older tree trunks are twisted and bent. Apple and orange trees flourish. Goats on farms bleat at us as we pass. Pass forests thick with tall pine trees.

Our first stop is at an ancient church with fading icons. It is gloomy inside the church, except for the flicker of candlelight. To my astonishment, pride of place is a dried old human hand in a glass cabinet. It belonged to saint someone, not sure who. No one else feels it is odd to have a petrified hand displayed. They take it in their stride. Alan's eyes widen when he sees the stiff hand.

An elderly, wrinkled woman, bent with arthritis, dressed in black from head to foot, glares from the back of the church. She is the protector and keeps a ferocious eye on everyone who enters the church. Perhaps she is there to prevent the glass cabinet from being broken and someone making off with the precious withered hand.

Renulla tells a story about my grandfather. He climbed the roof of this same church fixing loose tiles. He, as the story goes, lost his balance and fell through the roof. Apparently, an angel dressed in white light guided his safe descent to the ground. He landed on his feet and sustained neither scratches nor broken bones. The church protector woman at the back jumps up and runs towards us; she adds a little more to the story.

"He saw the angel with his own eyes," she said and pointed to the ceiling. "He fell from there and she supported him on the way down."

I stare at the ceiling, now covered with Byzantine paintings of Jesus and his disciples. Try to visualise the event. Falling through the roof and being guided by a white light. The story passed from one generation to the next, a much-loved tale.

Mother nods, she has heard this story before.

I translate to Alan, he shakes his head.

Mother furiously kisses every icon she can reach, lights several candles, murmurs endless prayers. Renulla does this too. I am not too keen to kiss the icons as I do not know who kissed the glass before me. Do a type of air kiss, cross myself, and light a candle, watch it flicker and move. Am about to take the obligatory photo, hold the camera to my face aimed at the ceiling where grandfather fell through the roof.

The old lady rushes from the back, waving her hands at me, shouting, "No photos, no photos."

Put the camera down, am shocked. Notice Renulla whisper loudly into the old woman's ear.

"These people are from Australia," she said pointing to Alan and me. "They came all this way to see this church. They are going back to Australia soon."

The old woman shrugs her shoulders, looks around at the other people in the church.

"I will turn away now and will not see you taking a photo," she said in a low voice to me.

"Thank you," I said.

I hand her money, which she counts, folds neatly and places in her apron pocket. She nods to me and goes back to her spot at the back of the church.

~

The next stop is Michael's sister's home, who is a smiling, gentle woman, middle-aged, and hospitable. Mother and I like her immediately. She embraces Renulla, Michael, and Taci warmly. Invites us to sit outside under the shade of two magnificent gnarled walnut trees in the courtyard. They have pride in the garden. The trees have been privy to hundreds of conversations and gossip.

It is a warm, lazy day, perfect for sitting under a magnificent walnut tree. There is a large orchard at the back. Whenever Michael visits his sister, he tends the orchard which contains established lemon, orange, and fig trees, laden with fruit. His sister is a widow; I am unsure how her husband died.

Taci, Mother, Renulla, and Michael and his sister share stories of the past. I have a photo of us seated around the table. Mother is happy in this photo, looks younger than her age. Renulla smiles, Michael laughs, Taci grins. Alan, Michael's sister and I stand behind them. A festive moment captured on film.

We nibble black olives and feta cheese, sip strong, brewed coffee. Later we stroll through the nearby long grass, check the vacant land littered with tumbled buildings. Land is scarce; people take the gift of land seriously. Each vacant block belongs to a family. We are told to watch out for snakes, step carefully, but see none.

Locate yet another church that has special meaning for Mother. The old church is small, preserved well, Byzantine style and cherished.

"Grandmother lived in Verga," Mother said. "I loved to stay with her. She was kinder to me than my own Mother."

She took out a handkerchief and blew her nose. "Grandmother and I prayed at this church at Easter." She gestures to the church.

"One year an angel visited the church congregation while we were praying." She blew her nose again. "I was about eight years old and felt the feathers from the angel wings as it flew past me," Mother said.

I have heard this story before. Now hear it in the context of the actual church.

Angels in your mist, you couldn't ask for more.

We stroll to Mother's grandmother's home. It is in ruins now with overgrown grass and another sturdy walnut tree. Mother peers through the ruins of what were bedrooms.

"This is where I slept when I stayed with

Grandmother, "she said, pointing to a small square of rubble. Her voice breaks.

The roof has broken long ago. Weeds grow from the floor. Broken wooden beams that separated rooms stand vigilant. Everything else destroyed.

"She was so good to me," Mother said, her voice as soft as a whisper.

"I was unhappy in my own home. But Grandmother spoilt me. She always hugged me and called me 'little Ekaterini.'" Her eyes moisten, voice trails off. She notices we are all quiet and watching her.

"That was so long ago," she said, looking uncomfortable.

I link arms with Mother, hug her.

We stop at another house, Mother's second cousin lives here, also named Ekaterini. Her daughter and granddaughter rush out of the door to meet us. They have heard of our arrival in Verga. Mother is again celebrated. Kisses and hugs, sugared sweets and glasses of cold water and coffee brought out. The daughter speaks English and converses with Alan which he appreciates.

Later, back at Michael's sister's house, we resume the earlier conversations. Michael's sister has a dark-haired daughter Mary with twins, a boy and a girl. She darts around making coffee, preparing dessert, providing cool drinks and disappears.

Army trucks whizz by, loaded with young soldiers, the army camp is close by.

I notice that Alan is pale. Even though the party is still going on, I make the decision to take Mother and Alan home in one of the taxis. Taci and Renulla and Michael intend to stay until late.

"Thank you for a wonderful time," I said. "I will send copies of the photos."

"Goodbye, thank you." Mother holds each one's hands and hugs them. She stares into their faces as if trying to capture their faces to memory.

Mother and Alan fall asleep in the taxi going back to The Hotel Blue Sea. When we reach our destination, I put them to bed.

Think of the miracles of the day. After my father died, only Mother and my two brothers were family. Since arriving in Mytilene, I have discovered many lovely people related to me.

CHAPTER 28

More relatives

Mytilene

Wed 16th June

I am perched on the white balcony; the passenger ferry has not arrived yet. There is a bandage over my right thumb. Yesterday, I accidentally sliced my thumb with a penknife that I used to cut an orange. Not sure if it needs sutures, so visited the pharmacist who bandaged it.

I collect an assortment of food from the hotel buffet for breakfast, place the food carefully on the tray and carry it to our rooms for Mother and Alan. Yesterday was a tiring day for both, they are still exhausted. They ate breakfast, both returned to bed. Alan is still struggling with the remnants of his flu.

Use this opportunity to deliver the photos of our visit to Thyra Street to the woman who bought the home. She smiles widely when she sees me at the door.

"Come in, come in," she said.

"Where is your Mother?"

"Sleeping, she is very tired. We have been visiting relatives in Verga," I said.

She nods, clings to her husband's hand as she speaks. Hand her the photos. She drops his hand momentarily to hold the photos. He has his chance. Bolts for the cobbled road. We chase after him and catch him.

"Got you," she said.

He laughs, it is a game for him.

I return to the hotel, check the state of our finances and forward expenses for the Hotel Blue Sea. Am mortified to learn that I cannot pay the hotel bill with my credit card as I had planned. For some reason, the hotel does not have credit card facilities. Calculate the balance using the traveller's cheques I have left. It is going to be close. We won't be able to afford to stay here much longer. I am furious with myself that I did not check if the hotel took credit cards. I assumed all hotels did.

Ring Taci, I tell him of our predicament, he knows of a few cheaper hotels in Mytilene that also take American Empress. I need to check them out. We could stay with Renulla. However, Mother would never cope with the very steep stairs.

Taci and I discuss plans for our return to Athens. "I insist you stay with me in Athens," he said.

"The only problem is that there are some steps from the street to the front door. Do you think your Mother will be able to do this? The steps are not steep."

It sounds a good solution and we are very grateful for his generosity.

~

Cousin Calliope collects us at 7 p.m. for sweets at her magnificent marbled home. The pink silk drapes flow from the ceiling to the floor. Elegant marble statues depicting ancient Greek athletes adorn the hallway. We are seated around a long, highly polished wooden table. Calliope has a worried look on her face, as though afraid something bad is about to happen. She is hospitable, delightful to us, especially to Mother. One daughter Clarie has twin daughters. Clara's husband works at the airport and sits next to Alan, speaks English with him.

Calliope's husband is short and dark. He is sharp and makes nasty comments about one of his daughters in front of us. The daughter looks away, her face flaming. She does not say anything. Perhaps is conditioned to the humiliation. Diamondu, the grandmother, could be a symbol of all Greek grandmothers. She has long, grey hair tied in a bun, wears a grey-and-white crotched shawl, frail and tiny, about the same age as Mother and they have much in common as they know each other well, being sisters-in-law.

The dining table is laden with delicious sweets; halva, kourabiethes, walnut cake, baklava. This is followed by aromatic Greek coffee. Several conversations melt into each other.

I couldn't put my finger on what precisely, but notice Mother acting strangely. She picks at her lips more often, stares in the distance, and does not say much. Was she upset, perhaps jealous of her sister-in-law living in this mansion with daughter Calliope? Or is it something else?

Mother pulls my sleeve and says, “It’s time to go.” A few minutes later she whispers, “Time to go as Alan is unwell.”

She is using him as an excuse.

Alan is laughing, having a great time chatting with Kostas who speaks in English.

She stands up and says, “We have to go now.”

Clarie drives us back to the Blue Sea Hotel. She stops on the way to point out cheaper hotels which take credit cards.

Mother is silent, replaying something horrible from the past in her head. I have concerns about her mental state.

We are scheduled to return to Callioppe’s on Friday for a meal.

CHAPTER 29

Hotel Erato

Mytilene

June 1993

This time, I am writing from the Hotel Erato balcony. We moved here yesterday. Paid the bill at the Blue Sea Hotel with the remaining traveller's cheques. We hated to leave the hotel as it suited us perfectly; lovely comfortable rooms, great views, clean, staff friendly.

"We are in the process of fixing up credit card facilities," the manager said when I explained why we were leaving.

"But everything takes time. We are sorry to lose you and your husband and Mother." The three of us have been a familiar fixture to the staff and other guests.

"Come back one day and have a drink at the bar," he said.

The manager knew the move to the Hotel Erato would disappoint. The rooms are pokey, noisy with a clattering air conditioner that blows warm air. But there is a lift for Mother.

Mother is annoyed with me that we moved

from the Blue Sea Hotel. “I liked it there,” she said, crossing her arms.

“So, did I, but we can’t afford it anymore,” I said.

“The Erato has no stars,” said Alan.

“It will do; it is clean, and we have no choice,” I said.

A busy construction site teeming with workers with jackhammers are next to the Hotel Erato. If you open the door to the balcony to cool the room, the hammering, banging, machines scream, men calling out to each other deafens. The men work from 3:30 a.m. under arc lights when it is cooler. If I close the door to block the noise out, I swelter in the heat of the room.

Despite all this, it is a pleasant morning. Have a view of my beloved sea, today is covered in soft pink hue. Nearby little birds chirp their little hearts out.

~

Yesterday I attempted to extend my credit limit with American Express but could not do so from the American Express agency on the island. The manager politely informed me that I must go to Athens branch.

“We are a small branch; you must process credit card extensions in Athens,” he said.

Taci is returning home to Athens tomorrow. He gossips about Calliope’s family. She has four children, two who have been problematic and do not live on the island. Taci said that at one time, one daughter disappeared when she married a French man and had a child. The marriage broke down, and she returned to her family on the island without the husband or child. The father of the child has full custody of the child. This is the daughter that Calliope's father was rude to when we were at their house. The other daughter Clarie. Married to Kostas.

"I will tell you more in Athens," he said.

Another jigsaw puzzle piece.

In the afternoon, we stroll to Renulla's home; one of her neighbours has exciting news.

"Your brother Yannis is alive and lives in the island of Cephalonia," she said to Mother.

"I thought he was dead," said Mother shaking her head.

"I have his phone number here," the neighbour passes a small piece of paper with Yannis's phone number.

"Ring him now," she said to me, pointing to Renulla's phone.

"Ring him," said Renulla, holding the phone.

Notice that Mother is not the least bit excited about learning Yannis is alive. Her face clouds over, is dark and brooding; as though a storm cloud obliterated the sunshine.

The coaxing from Renulla and the neighbour continues.

I dial the number. Take a deep breath.

"Hello, I am the daughter of your sister Ekaterini

and her husband Michael Evangelou from Australia. My Mother, husband, and I are in Lesvos." I said.

Silence. I repeat my words.

Yannis is suspicious, guarded. I expected this response.

Attempt small talk. "It is hot in Mytilene? How are you and your wife?" I asked. "I will ring you tomorrow and we can speak again."

Renulla is overjoyed that Mother and Yannis will be reunited after forty-two years.

I know Yannis will check on the veracity of my call by contacting his contact in Mytilene, most likely Renulla's neighbour who gave us the phone number.

The next day when I ring, Yannis is a different man, warm and friendly.

"When can you come to Cephalonia and meet my wife and me? You must bring my beloved sister to see us," he said.

"I will let you know in a few days," I said. "I have some business to complete in Athens and will ring you."

I thought a chat over the phone would suffice for him, but his insistence that we come to his island is urgent and heartfelt.

"You must come. Please. I am an old sick man. It would make me happy to see my sister again," he said.

Put the phone to Mother's ear so she can speak to Yannis. She shows no emotion nor pleasure, nods her head, says a few words and hands the phone back to me.

I was expecting some excitement to speak to her brother after forty-two years' absence.

But there is none.

CHAPTER 30

Ayvalik

Turkey

June 1993

Much excitement; today Alan and I are catching the ferry to Ayvalik, Turkey. It sounds so exotic to say that. I am looking forward to it. We drop Mother at Renulla's at the agreed time. She is thrilled to spend a day with Renulla and her friends. They have serious girl talk to do. In my mind's eye, I see the women bending close saying, "Oh no," or "Fancy that," as lives and people are discussed.

Mother and Renulla are both horrified we have chosen to visit Turkey.

"I would never set foot on Turkish soil," said Renulla.

"No Turk would get any money from me," said Mother, her voice rising in volume.

Their memories still too sharp to forget the long and violent history between Greece and Turkey; time has not healed the rift. The stories of brutality and war punched up to the present. To Alan and me, Turkey is an exotic faraway place to be explored, nothing more.

Lesvos faces Ayvalik, a seaside town on the Northwest Aegean coast of Turkey. Apparently, as I am told, after the collapse of the Ottoman Empire, many Ottoman Greeks from Ayvalik moved to Greece and Turkish citizens moved to Ayvalik. The town has been in turmoil for centuries, controlled by Turkey and Greece in turn. The Greek army took over Ayvalik in 1919, and it was returned to Turkey by Turkish forces in1922 under the forces of Mustafa Kemal Ataturk. Some Greeks escaped to Greece at the time, others were seized by the Turkish Army and many died in death marches to Anatolia. Some of the victims were Christian clergy and the local bishop.

Many of the Turkish mosques once were Greek Orthodox churches, now converted into Muslim structures.

I am distracted listening to war stories, time runs away with us. We sprint to the ferry *Erron*. We dash up the gangplank with minutes before it pulls out. Am still puffing as I walk around the ferry surveying the other passengers. They appear to be a mixed lot, Greek shoppers in search of a bargain, and young holiday makers. A young Greek/Australian couple tell me they are travelling to Turkey for a short break away from the husband's demanding Greek family.

"I don't like Lesvos. I want to go back to Australia," said the young blonde woman. "My in-laws cried and demanded we return to Lesvos. They pretended they were sick and dying. They are healthier than I am and will live to 100." She shakes her head.

"In the end, we did return to Lesvos. It was the worst decision." She crosses her arms and gives a sigh.

"Nothing I do is right. My mother-in-law nags me from morning to night." She blows air at her hanging blonde fringe.

He nods his head. "Once you experience freedom, it is hard to go back to prison. You and your husband are fortunate to go back to Australia. I wish we could go back with you."

It shocks me to hear this. Lesvos is an enchanted island with delightful people to me. Obviously, there is another side that I have not thought about.

Ayvalik, as other tourist towns, teems with bustling crowds. People mingle along the waterside, eat at the open-air restaurants, swim and sail. The port is massive, yachts and sailboats dot the water. The Seven Brothers restaurant next to the harbour is our choice for lunch. The restaurant is run by the mother and father and their seven sons. It turned out to be an excellent choice. The food is tasty; succulent, grilled lamb kababs, threaded with red peppers and onions. Assorted salads. Thick aromatic muddy coffee with sticky baklava. The food is similar to Greek food.

Ayvalik is a market town. Shopkeepers, eager to

sell, step into our path hassling us to buy at every turn. It can be frightening; persistent shopkeepers followed us down the road demanding we return to their shop and buy from them. At one stage, we ducked into a coffee shop and hid from one persistent shopkeeper who trailed us down the street. He wouldn't take no for an answer. Later, we find a less aggressive shopkeeper and spend on gifts for Renulla and the others; mostly leather wallets and bags. Leather is cheap and plentiful. A nice touch is the refreshing glass of sweet black tea that is handed to us as we enter.

The rug shops are truly impressive; dazzling carpets in a kaleidoscope of colours and patterns—any size rug or carpet can be made, any pattern, any colour. The shopkeepers can package the carpet of your choice and post it to your country. We watch two Turkish women weave a beautiful carpet by hand, turning fingers in and out, threading coloured thread through the weave.

I wondered about repetitive strain injury, notice both women have bent and deformed fingers.

We do not buy any rugs.

I wish we had longer at Ayvalik, perhaps stay for a week. We could have explored the ancient cities of Assos, Troy to the north and Pergamon to the east. I have read a number of books about the historical significance of these towns. Mount Ida is important in Greek mythology and the cult of Cybele, the Trojan War and the epic poem *The Iliad* from Homer. Various archaeological sites prove that Ayvalik was inhabited from the prehistoric times.

However, must make do with one-day sightseeing.

There is a cultural mix for the women. Some Muslim women are fully covered with headscarves and wear long nondescript overcoats. Other Turkish women wear bright Western dress and no scarves.

A watermelon seller with a cart laden with huge green watermelons peddles his ware. He cuts a watermelon in front of us; the sweet smell brings people to taste and buy. Fresh watermelon on a hot day is perfect. He calls out "fresh watermelons," and instantly a crowd mills around and the cart. It was soon empty.

Later, catch the ferry for Mytilene, watch the sun set over the ocean, the sky red and yellow, magnificent.

Collect Mother from Renulla's.

"Did you enjoy the day?" I said.

I had a wonderful time." Mother said.

"What did you talk about?" I said.

"Secrets," she said and giggled.

CHAPTER 31

Saint Theodore

Mytilene

June 1993

Renulla's son Nikos and wife Narcia have been nominated to show us more of the island.

"Would you like to go with Alan and Cally or stay with me for the day?" said Renulla to Mother.

"I want to stay with you," said Mother.

More secrets, I thought.

That settled, we leave with Nikos and his family.

Nikos is a tall dark man and has a video camera to record our day. Narcia is a bright woman with glossy, black hair. She has a degree in psychology but is not working now, instead bringing up their young son and daughter. Narcia and Nikos speak English well which pleases Alan. The children, Cleopatra and Michael, chatter and ask many questions. Little Michael is three and a half, and a live wire, Cleo more serious, is six. The children remind me of my own children about the same age.

"Would you like to go to Molyvos?" asked Narcia, turning from the front seat.

"What is at Molyvos?" Alan asked. He peered out of the window trying to get his bearings.

"Molyvos is the most picturesque place on Lesvos; tourists love the place. It has everything, beautiful beaches, entertaining taverns, even a castle," said Narcia.

"Nikos and I often drive there. The children love to play on the beach."

"At dusk, fishing boats set out in a line with their lanterns and nets," said Nikos.

We explored the Molyvos harbour on the outskirts of the village, it was as beautiful as Narcia suggested. Picturesque, cosmopolitan with many tavernas and a strong marine culture of fishing boats and nets. Here and there octopus hang to dry.

The castle stands guard over the area and built in the Byzantine period.

We stop at the Church of the Mermaid. Each church has a unique history and flavour. The churches are part of the patriotism of the region. Busloads of tourists disgorge from buses to see the oldest church in the region, more than 500 years old, has been damaged by earthquakes.

The Church of 114 Steps is perched high on a hill and has extensive sea views.

"Mother would have insisted on walking up the 114 steps to the church," I said.

Nikos locates an Old World restaurant with hanging purple wisteria vines and red geraniums in pots, perched very high on a hill. It felt like being in an aeroplane and looking at a city as you circle to land, the view expansive and breathtaking. The food is delicious; grilled lamb and horta (greens), roast potatoes, and Greek salad. Followed by strong coffee and sweets.

We stop at Mandamados at the Church of the Taxiarches again. I have a better view of the icon and light another candle remembering the story.

Lesvos is an amazing island, so much to discover.

We return to Renulla's at 7 p.m.

Alan said he was exhausted and returned to the Hotel Erato; still not well.

Renulla invited Mother and me to join them to watch the yearly procession of Saint Theodore's bones from one end of the island to the other. The town is bustling with humanity; people are in a carnival atmosphere. Young girls dressed as angels parade through the town followed by police and army marching bands. Priests file past in flowing black gowns and flat-topped hats. The head priests are dressed in ornate, gold-embroidered gowns. They hold ornate, gold boxes which contain the remains of Saint Theodore. When the procession and remains of Saint Theodore pass, everyone bows and crosses themselves.

"Many miracles happen each year when the procession goes past," said Renulla.

"The bones have miracle properties."

Nikos drives Mother and me back to the hotel.

Mother is elated, her face has a sheen of happiness, chatters nonstop.

"I am blessed to return to my island," she said.

CHAPTER 32

Getting to know you

Mytilene

June 1993

Today I visited the Mytilene Hospital on my own. I had organised an appointment with the matron. My background as a nursing academic has made me curious about nursing in Lesvos. I have formulated a few questions: How many years does it take to become a Greek nurse. Do nurses have a strong career ladder for promotion?

The matron is tall and imposing, wears a navy uniform with white collar. We discuss Australian and Greek nursing programs, the differences and similarities.

"Would you like a tour of the hospital?" she asked.

I did.

She escorts me around the hospital, pointing out special areas of interest.

"This is the birthing unit. No one is in labour," she said looking inside.

The surgical and medical wards are filled with patients and relatives. The operating theatre was empty. We pass the children's ward, outpatients, and emergency department.

The matron is obviously proud of her hospital and staff. It is very clean and well maintained. I speak with three young nurses; the Greek nursing course is a two-year diploma course. The Australian nursing course is three years, a degree course. The nurses ask me about Australia. They are curious about pay and conditions and are surprised to hear Australian nurses are held in high regard. Nursing is considered a low-status job in Greece.

The heat oppressive, I drip with sweat, my face beetroot red, I stop often to get my breath as I walk back to the hotel.

~

In the afternoon, Renulla, Mother, and I are on a sisterhood mission to visit another sister-in-law. Anna is a widow like all my Father's brothers' wives. She is American-born, a nurse, and speaks excellent English. Anna is bedridden, does not walk. A large black-and-white photo of Anna in an American nurse's uniform hangs on the wall. She is a handsome woman, no children, and cared by neighbours who are good to her.

I mention that I toured the hospital in the morning.

"Nursing at that hospital is of low standard," she said.

"Did you know that the nurses do not look after

the patients properly? The family has to wash and feed the patients." She bent over and whispered.

"If you want the nurses to look after your patient, you have to pay them money to receive proper care."

I am saddened.

Renulla accompanies us back to the hotel so we do not get lost again. I have not mastered the twisting roads and alleyways to the hotel Erato. It is in a complex part of the town, easy to become disorientated.

~

Later that night, we hire a taxi to Calliope's home; the taxi driver is new and becomes disorientated, and we arrive late.

Calliope has prepared a delicious banquet. Various meats like goat, lamb, beef, assorted fresh salads, several vegetables, potatoes, beans, and eggplant followed by a collection of cheese and bread, and aromatic coffee, sweets, and watermelon slices. I am aware of the time and effort made by Calliope to have everything perfect.

And it is.

Alan sits next to Kostas; they discuss airports and planes.

Mother is seated next to Diamondu, the grandmother, and appear in deep conversation.

"What did you do today?" asked Callioppe.

Mention my trip to the hospital and what Anna said about the hospital.

"The twins both suffer from asthma and require careful care and medical management. Both girls have spent time in the hospital with severe asthma attacks," said Clarie.

"I have found the hospital very helpful. No complaints from me."

I was pleased to hear this.

"Anna was a beautiful woman when she was younger," said Callioppe.

"When Anna's husband died, she preferred to stay in Mytilene than return to America." Callioppe passed me a plate of freshly cut watermelon.

"All the family keeps an eye on Anna. Renulla and I take turns to visit and do what needs doing; the neighbours are very good to her."

The food and evening were perfect, but I felt an undercurrent of anxiety from Mother. She looks uneasy.

CHAPTER 33

Our second last day

Mytilene

June 1993

It is Diamondu's name day and celebrations are planned for the ladies. Mother is invited, is relaxed about going to Callioppe's house as only women will be there. Also prearranged is an outing for Alan and me with Clarie and Kostas, to show us more of Lesvos.

I am aware Renulla and Calliope have been magnificent, organising their children to drive us to interesting places. We are extremely grateful for the generosity of their time and effort towards us.

Clarie is fair, slight of build, and friendly, whereas Kostas is tall, dark, and quieter. The twin brunette girls are beautiful little chatterboxes. Love this in little children; so much to say and so innocent. Clarie is an attentive and caring mother; Kostas a loving father.

Our first stop is a natural habitat of native turtles which live under a bridge. The twins throw pieces of bread and at once many turtles poke their heads out of the water and gobble the bread.

"I can count forty turtles," I said, very excited at seeing them.

Clarie points to a stork sitting in a huge nest which is perched on a high chimney.

"The owners cannot light their fire while the stork is sitting on the chimney," said Clarie.

The next destination, the Pebble Beach, stones so sharp they cut your feet if walk barefooted. Have my bathers and enjoy a bracing swim with the twins and Clarie and Kostas. Alan did not swim, the water too cold for his liking.

Lunch is another superb open-aired restaurant on the beach edge. Eating alfresco is my favourite way to eat. We order delicious fried fish and vegetables. I love the way meals are served with a variety of dishes to taste and experiment. Alan eats with a hearty appetite and has become quite adventurous, tasting a variety of Greek food such as eggplant, although he still draws the line at eating octopus.

Kostas drives us to a secret underground church, the entrance hidden from sight.

"When Turkey occupied Lesvos, the Turks forbade Christianity and closed all the churches," said Kostas.

"This little church enabled the Greeks to pray in secret."

We locate the entrance, step down the steep steps, to find a miniature church, with whitewashed walls and religious icons and of course candles.

Return to Claire and Kostas's home for coffee and cake. The house is on an upper level over Calliope's house. In Lesvos, it is common for homes to be built with three or more levels. Each child has a level, so they can live there when married and have a family. It is an excellent plan to assist with babysitting, and when old age and illness strikes, family is close by to assist. Their house is contemporary with comfortable furniture and modern paintings.

Kostas is a ham radio and electronics fan and has a room set up for his hobby.

"I fixed the radios for the hotel Erato," he said.

"The radio in our room works," I said.

He shows us his valuable coin collection, pre-Christian coins, a few dating back to the Roman times. An old urn encrusted with shells lies in a corner.

"My Father caught it in his fishing net," he said.

We sit companionly in the kitchen, light streaming in from the windows.

"Why did your Father leave Mytilene?" Clarie asks me.

"I am not sure..." I said.

What could I say? I am not sure that everything Taci has told me is true.

We collect Mother who is brimming with tales about the pleasurable day at Calliope's. The sisters-in-law explored shared experiences. One part of me would have loved to be a fly on the wall to listen.

“What did you two talks about?” I asked, giving her a hug.

“I can’t tell you, secrets...” she giggled.

~

We are flying to Athens the next day; Kostas checked our plane tickets for Athens. We have been given the wrong flight, not the later one as I requested. It is hard enough getting Mother organised in the mornings; an early flight would be impossible. Kostas and Alan make a mad scramble to the airport to change the times of departure.

Clarie takes Mother and me back to the hotel.

As soon as we enter the hotel room, the phone rings.

“Where are you?” asked Renulla.

“We are waiting for you at Nikos house.”

Explain about the tickets. Nikos collects us and drives us to his house. It is an elegant two-story home. Cleo’s room is girly and pink, her bed piled with stuffed toys. Young Michael has an interesting collection of planes and boats.

Nikos plays the video of the day of the day we toured the island with his family. It is professional with Zorba music and subtitles showing all the places we visited. Mother and I love it. It is a gift for us.

“Whenever we watch the video, it will bring us back to the wonderful warmth of the family and the beautiful experiences we have shared,” said Mother.

I nod. Am overcome with emotion, blow my nose.

We enjoy the cool of the evening in the garden under the clear sky and twinkling stars. At midnight, Nikos drives us back to the hotel.

Am sad for tomorrow we leave Mytilene and the family I have grown to love.

CHAPTER 34

Our last day in Mytilene

Mytilene

June 1993

Today is our last day in Mytilene, am in my usual spot writing on the balcony of the Erato Hotel. The construction team is going full pelt, "bang, bang." Male voices rise and fall in the early morning air.

Notice a police car with two policemen in uniform stop in the middle of the road, hazard lights on. One policeman runs in a small church, lights a candle, says a prayer. The other waits in the car. The police car blocks the road, a line of tooting cars behind him. In a minute or two, the police officer hurries out of the church and waves to the line of cars. They drive off.

Watch a procession of men and women pop into the church, light candles, heads bow in prayer, cross their chests, and leave. On this island, reverence for religion is universal.

Someone told me the population of Mytilene is around is 40,000. In my mind, there must be an equal number of cars and motor scooters. And several million olive trees; apparently, someone counted the olive trees.

The day is already sweltering hot, my skin prickles with heat. The ferry boat has docked in the port; cars rumble off the ferry. A policeman blows his whistle, directs traffic left and right. The town bustles; cars, motor bikes, scooters, buses moving as one.

I have many things on my 'to do list' today.

Go downstairs and pay the hotel bill, try not to gasp at the cost. Taci rings from Athens to confirm our flight to Athens.

"Hurry up and come to Athens, we will pick you up from the airport." Taci said.

I am looking forward to spending more time with Taci and meet his brother Panayiotis and his wife and family. I expect they are like Renulla's family—hospitable and delightful. Hopefully, he will have more to tell me about my Father.

Am hyper-excited. "Settle down," I tell myself, but cannot.

I wonder about Alan, could he be stressed by the trip? Does he feel powerless and dragged along? I discard that thought, that idea. And hope by ignoring it does not come back to bite me.

All I see is the next potential shining gem of the next stage of the journey ahead.

~

For the last time, we find our way to Renulla's house. The path and the houses are familiar to us now. Wild buttercups under trees, brilliant red tulips, and purple wisteria flowers draped over a fence, a willowy gum tree.

Our last meal together is delicious; stuffed tomatoes and grilled eggplant and salad. Ice cream for dessert and strong coffee.

How to repay a woman who has done so much, introduced us to everyone, and entertained us? This woman made everything happen, quietly simply in her lovely way. Renulla's home has been an oasis to us. We have been made welcome, fed, and loved.

Gifts are exchanged. I bought leather handbags, wallets for everyone from our ferry trip to Turkey, whiskey for Michael. They, in turn, shower us with delicate embroidered table clothes depicting maps of Lesvos.

I distribute more copies of photos of our shared times, have spent a fortune on developing and printing, but it brings great pleasure.

The wonderful sound of family. I smile from ear to ear. Have searched for this closeness all my life. Here it is. But am aware it will be over soon. I will remember the feeling of being part of something greater.

Because of Renulla we met the extended family. We have visited new places, had a wonderful time. The fact my mother is beaming with happiness is because of Renulla.

I will miss you Renulla, am honoured to be part of your beautiful loving family. Dad would be smiling from wherever he is.

What did Khalil Gibran say? All happiness has a kernel of sadness at its core. Happiness and sadness sit together.

~

At 3:30 p.m., Nikos drives us to the airport. Clarie and the twins are also there to see us off. Mum lights a final candle at the church at the airport.

I cannot see for crying, my glasses fogged. Am astounded that I have become so emotional. It comes from somewhere that has not been expressed before. Mother cries and hugs Renulla, will not let her go. She has been a talisman for the happy times Mother spent before Australia. Even Alan has moist eyes.

This trip was originally for Mother's benefit, but I reclaimed my Greek heritage.

The plane circles over Lesvos, grip the seat with one hand and hold Mother's hand with the other. Neither of us speak.

Have no idea what she is thinking.

I watch the island become smaller and smaller until it is a speck and we are in blue sky. I look over at Alan; he is reading the brochures in his seat pocket.

Goodbye, family, I never knew you existed a few weeks back. And now you will always be part of me. Will I ever see you again?

CHAPTER 35

Staying with Taci

Athens

June 1993

Athens airport is covered in a haze of heat and dust. Looks almost surreal. We circle once, twice, three times before we land. The reality hits me, masses of people trying to find where they are going, again the airport chaos.

"Don't leave me," Mother said, clings to me, is unnerved by the noise, people pushing.

Taci and Antoniou (Renulla's son) are at the airport waiting for us. Bless them.

The streets of Athens are chocked with honking cars and the pungent smell of dust and gasoline. The heat falls on us like a heavy blanket. We are sweating profusely. Arrive at Taci's apartment. Alan and I put our arms around Mother and help her up the steps to Taci's door. Is unsteady, hope we don't have to go up and down the steps too often.

Taci shares his home with his son Vasilis, has two dogs, trained as watchdogs. One huge brown dog shows his yellow teeth at me in a menacing welcome. The other a timid, white French poodle hides under a chair when he sees us. It is clear the dogs own the apartment and pad around as masters of the domain. The bigger dog has a terrifying bark that sends shivers into my soul and reverberates throughout the apartment.

"The big dog is trained to attack on command," Taci said, a matter of fact.

I don't doubt it. He sniffs around me and is engaged in a personal quest to trip me, using his bulk. He pads in front and turns suddenly, and I trip over him. He does not like us. He periodically shows his teeth to make a point. The feeling is mutual. Mother and I are fearful as to what he might do apart from barking. The little dog is quieter and steps out of our way. It can't be much of a life for the dogs. They are cooped up inside. Am not sure if they are taken for walks. The dogs wander around the prized art and artefacts as kings in a manor.

Taci's place is crammed with fine antique furniture, the walls covered with large modern abstract paintings; they look expensive. Chaos and class thrown together, is a fascinating apartment and like Taci, has layers of intrigue.

Taci's brother Panayiotis welcomes us. Mother greets him warmly, recognises him but I do not. He lives in the apartment below Taci with his wife Petra and son Michael.

We unpack, nibble on olives and cheese. Taci tugs two photo albums from the massive bookshelves that line the lounge room walls. He points out several photos of my Father with his brothers and parents.

"See how handsome your Father was," Taci said.

Father is young, straight-backed. The family appears close; I have been named after the Mother Calliope. The sister Harikula (mother of Renulla) is the only girl.

"The brothers were ruthless in their search for wealth," said Taci, stares at the photo of his Father.

"Several brothers became very wealthy," he said. "My father was ruthless and wealthy." He stopped, still looking at the photo. "I am sorry to say my father was not a nice man," his face had a down-turned expression.

We are enthralled with his stories, he tells the most amazing tales.

"Don't believe everything Taci tells you," Mother said in a low voice when I take her to the toilet. "He exaggerates."

I want the stories to be true.

At 10 p.m., Taci decides to drive us to a local restaurant; his brother joins us.

The streets are less congested, cooler, a lovely Athenian evening.

The head waiter of the restaurant greets Taci.

"Good evening Taci; good to see you again. Do you want your usual table?"

We are seated in a quiet spot of the restaurant, ready for a fine meal, Mother is hungry, so is Alan.

Plates of sliced lamb, dolmades land on the

table, followed by baked potatoes, grilled eggplant, endive, olives, and cheese. We eat like hungry lions. Again, mop the juices with slabs of thick bread.

Notice that bottle after bottle of retsina ends up next to Taci. He pours himself drink after drink. Panayiotis, Alan, Mother and I sip at our one glass of retsina. Petra is at work, is a travel representative.

Taci becomes loud and annoying, criticising his brother, and needling him unmercifully about politics.

"You were a German sympathiser," he said.

"Otherwise you would not have married a German woman."

"You are an idiot, Taci," Panayiotis argues back.

"You were on the side of the Germans," said Taci.

"No, I was not."

Taci is strident. Insults fly back and forth between the brothers.

Alan, Mother, and I are unnerved and try to change the topic.

"How is Vasilis?" said Mother, bending towards Taci.

Taci will not be distracted.

"Panayiotis was a German sympathiser because he married a German," he said.

He is on a roll and aims to harm his brother in front of us. This is galling for us. What happened to the gentle, elegant man in Mytilene? Has he turned into a rude bore?

The night descends into farce. Horrible insults bounce off each brother.

"I have had enough," said Panayiotis. He stands, face red with anger.

He throws money on the table to pay for his share of the bill and storms off into the night leaving us with a drunk.

Taci continues filling his glass and drinking, is bellicose and belligerent. We try every trick in the book to go home for Mother's sake. She is wide-eyed and mute.

Wish I had known that Taci was like this, we would never have stayed with him. Am irritable; Alan shaking with powerless fury.

"Mother is old and needs her sleep," I repeated.

I manage to make Taci leave, but he insists on driving home.

"Let's take a taxi to your place," I suggested.

"I can drive," he hisses.

Mother mumbles, crosses herself, and throws her arms in the air. I feel for sure we will be killed by this madman. Force Alan to sit in the front seat to try to manage Taci who is acting like an idiot, running through red lights, weaving on the road, turning to talk to me and Mother, not concentrating on driving.

"Taci, the light is red," I shout.

"The light is only a little bit red," Taci said.

By good fortune, we return to Taci's home in one piece. It has been a terror ride. Alan and I carry a panicked Mother up the steps. Try everything in my power to calm her, she shouts, cries, bangs her head with her hands.

"It is all your fault," she shouts at me.

Eventually, drag her to bed. She has reverted to form. She is mumbling loudly to herself, picking furiously at her lips.

I say a prayer of thanks for our safe return. All those candles in Mytilene must have borne fruit.

"I blame you for this," Alan said poking at my chest.

His voice is mean and menacing. He blames me for the fiasco at the restaurant because we are staying at Taci's.

It is humiliating to be abused by my husband, in my cousin's house.

Taci falls silent, says "Goodnight," and flops fully clothed on the divan.

During the night, Mother calls me to take her to the toilet. The dogs jump up as soon as they hear us, growl as we pass. Mother shrieks.

How could I know the Taci in Mytilene is a different man to the one in Athens? Taci demanded we stay with him. We are in no financial position to pay for a hotel. How could I have known that Taci is a mean drunk and has attack dogs?

I sit on the balcony, darkness envelopes me, dodge the dogs waiting to trip me as I go to bed.

~

In the morning, breakfast cereal and bread are laid out for us. Taci is nowhere to be found. The dogs trail us, sniff our backsides. I hate this. I do everything I can to separate Mother from the dog; she screams whenever they came near. At one stage, I close the door on them on the balcony and we move around in peace. The dogs bark their displeasure.

A few hours later, Taci arrives carrying a tray of stuffed tomatoes and is his cheerful Mytilene self. There are no remnants of the Taci from last night.

Later in the day, Alan, Taci, and I make plans to go to the American Express office in Athens. It is a distance from Taci's home. Mother will stay home. We will use a taxi as parking is difficult. The plan is for Taci to introduce us to the Manager of American Express and assist with the language. I need to obtain an advance on my American Express card, extend it. Alan demanded I do the advance in my name. He is still angry with me. I bite my tongue. Athens is not the time to stir him up. He is likely to lash out, emotions and tiredness running ahead of good sense.

"I don't want to stay here by myself," Mother said. She is indignant, hands on hips.

"You won't be able to cope with the long walk, and there are many steps to the American Express office," said Taci, his voice gentle.

"And it is very hot outside."

"No, I will not stay here with the dogs," Mother said. "You might leave me here and never come back."

"I promise you on the head of your brother-in-law, my father, that I will come back for you." He speaks gently to her.

"I will ask Panayiotis to come in at five if we are not back."

This comforts her a little and she agrees to stay. We close the bedroom door so the dogs don't come in and annoy her.

"We will be right back," I said.

I never thought what might happen if we had an accident and died and never made it back. Sometimes you never think of the consequences. I was focussed on the main problem of the need for money.

American Express turns out to be a definitive exercise in pain and embarrassment. Not only because of my poor Greek, but worse, treated badly because I was female. The manager refused to acknowledge me, only speaking to Alan or Taci. Invisible in his eyes. Taci was angry at my treatment, demanded to speak to the senior manager.

I need money to take Mother to see her brother in Cephalonia and pay for accommodation. Am aware this might be the last time Mother will see her brother. This trip is a chance to fix things between the two of them.

And need to pay for any other expenses until our return to Australia.

Eventually, we are done. But not until American Express rings Australia twice to confirm my employment and everything I said was true. They softened their approach when they discovered I was an academic in a well-known university and then, only then, treated me with respect.

My credit card limit is extended immediately.

I sigh with relief.

Taci has things to do, hands me the key to his apartment so we can let ourselves in. Alan and I return by taxi, starved and rattled.

When we reach Taci's door, the key does not open the front door. I try. Alan tries. It slips into the latch but does not turn. Now what?

Mother calls "Cally, Cally," when she hears my voice. The attack dogs bark up a storm; they think we are breaking into the house. The whole suburb must have heard them, panic and noise overlapping.

As if on cue, Taci arrives with a huge tray of more food for us.

"Oops, I forgot to tell you, you need pliers to turn the lock." He pulls a small plier from his pocket and turns the key. The door opens.

I laugh, more in frustration than humour. Everything about Taci is extraordinary.

Mother is a mess, agitated, has been picking at her lips, created a nasty gash which bleeds from the bottom lip. She mutters obscenities at me.

"You deliberately left me here alone, so the dogs could kill me," she said, shaking her fist at me.

On the plus side, she is alive and not ripped to shreds by the attack dogs.

Thank you, God.

We eat the delicious food. I breathe out.

~

Later, Petra and Panayiotis visit. Petra speaks in perfect English, is charming, thin with mischievous blue eyes. I warm to her at once. She apologises for Taci and her husband arguing the night before.

"They always fight," Petra said.

"They drink too much and then fight. They are still boys at heart. But they love each other. Unfortunately, I had to work late and could not come with you. If I am with them, I stop the fights."

Petra, Panayiotis, Taci, Mother, Alan, and I squash together in Taci's small, white kitchen. The stuffed peppers, eggplant, and roast potatoes are delicious. The dogs circle around us.

The conversation turns to travel. Petra said she can obtain great discounts for us for a seven-day cruise trip that travels to the religious sites in the Mediterranean. It is called The Alexandrian Egypt/Holy Land Cruise and departs from Piraeus, stops at Port Said (Cairo), Ashdod (Jerusalem/Bethlehem), Limassol (Cyprus), Rhodes, Kusadasi (Ephesus) Patmos. Then back to Piraeus. The cruise boat is called *MTS Odysseus*, part of the Epirotiki line. Petra said the service is fantastic.

"I can obtain discounted travel agent tickets for you," she said.

"Are you interested?" She smiled.

"I cannot use the tickets so am giving you the opportunity to use them."

Our eyes widen. We have the American Express money.

Mother has dreamed of going to Cairo, Jerusalem, Bethlehem and Patmos. We have talked about it over the years.

"One day, I will take you to Greece and Jerusalem," I used to say as a child.

Mother is almost jumping for joy at the prospect.

"Let's go," she said.

The only problem is the cruise starts this Friday. It is Wednesday today. Can we manage Cephalonia and the cruise? We discuss the options, the consensus is, "Let's do it," hang the expense.

I ring Yannis, Mother's brother in Cephalonia, and tell him we can visit for two days.

"This is wonderful news. You must stay with us. I can't believe that I will see Ekaterini after all these years. I have waited over forty years for this," he said, his voice breaking with emotion.

Yannis tells me he once came to Melbourne to search for my mother. He had been told by the renters that she had died. The house in Springvale was rented during that time when Mother and

John and Jim lived on the farm in Taggerty. No wonder Yannis had been guarded when I rang from Mytilene. Yannis is the last surviving member of Mother's direct family.

I share the information with Mother expecting her to be excited, but she has the familiar absent look on her face. I wonder why?

~

That night Taci unravels more surprising stories. He is an engaging storyteller. We study his photo albums again; people long gone, and events of significance become real. Alan listens, I translate. Mother adds bits to Taci's stories.

"I miss my wife so much," he said his eyes full tears.

"She had cancer and we had the best doctors and surgeons in Athens." He shakes his head.

"They were powerless to stop the cancer." He blows his nose. "No one could save her; the cancer killed her."

We are silent.

"I hate my Father," Taci added.

Am surprised at the hatred he harbours for his own father.

He tells us he caught his father trying to seduce his wife. His wife was terrified.

"Taci's father was a disgusting, horrible man," Petra said, placing emphasis on disgusting.

"Thankfully both brothers take after their mother."

"I used to have problems with alcohol after my wife died," Taci said, as though this was something long ago. He mentions a cousin with narcotic problems.

Maybe the cousin tried to rob him and that is the purpose for the attack dogs.

"I have this gun for protection," Taci said, pulling a small silver revolver out of a drawer.

Alan's eyes pop at the sight of the gun. He has never experienced anything like Taci's household.

"My daughter does not talk to me because of my girlfriend. The daughter wants me in mourning all my life." Taci said.

"It is time to go to bed," I said to Mother and Alan. They look overwhelmed.

I cannot sleep, too much percolating in my mind. Wash our clothes, hang them on the balcony line, and dodge the dogs. Drink in the city lights.

I am in Athens, the fabulous city of history.

~

The next day I pay for our tickets to Cephalonia and the cruise, using American Express. I am very appreciative for the delightful Petra and her travel agent discount.

Later, a small man delivers the Cephalonia tickets to Taci's door. He refuses to come inside, terrified of Taci's attack dogs who bark furiously when they hear him.

I hire a taxi to collect the tickets for the cruise. The driver speaks perfect English and is a safe driver. Alan stays behind with Mother and she is rescued from the ordeal of the steps and the attack dogs.

Taci's son, Vasilis arrives home. He is twenty-five years old, jet black hair, friendly, handsome, young Greek man. He is curious about us. His English is good; he engages Alan, asks him about his work as a flight engineer. It is obvious that Taci and his son share a deep affection for each other.

A steady stream of people come and go from Taci's place.

The visitors are respectful towards Mother; I am touched by the reverence she generates. To be old in Greece is a great honour. Better than in Australia.

The chaos and loveliness sit side by side.

Taci is slighted when I attempt to contribute for our stay and food. We have taken over Taci's room, Mother is in the spare room. Taci does not complain about sleeping on the divan in the lounge room.

~

I write this in Taci's apartment. It is hot, blistering hot outside. The street covered in a thick heat haze. It is well above forty degrees. The locals manage their lives around the heat. Rest when it is hottest. Eat and live when it is cooler at night.

Everyone seems to smoke in Greece; his apartment reeks of cigarette smoke.

In the cool of the evening, Alan, Mother, and I stroll around the block. It is a classy neighbourhood, expensive, well-heeled. There are limits on how tall an apartment can be and there are no high-rise buildings. On the ground, it feels like a village. White perfumed gardenias are everywhere; geraniums in barrels and pots. Every square inch that has space has a flower or plant. Small shops are located at every corner; sweet shops, delicatessen, fruit shops and they stay open until late at night.

We meet Panayiotis and Petra, return to the apartment together.

"I have paid for the tickets for the cruise," I said.

"Thank you so much."

"Enjoy, my darling," Petra said.

Organise Mother for bed; she is disorientated in Taci's house. It is quite dark inside and strange. Alan is tired, goes to bed too.

When Taci returns, am invited to join his delightful friends. The couple have recently become engaged. I have reservations about being in the way and plan to sneak off to bed at the first opportunity. They refuse to let me go, ask questions about Australia. To them, Australia seems exotic and far away, twenty-four hours in an aeroplane.

CHAPTER 36

Somewhere in the sky

June 1993

We are seated comfortably in an ATR seventy-two-seater plane. Alan in front, Mother and I behind. We fly over the Peloponnese to Cephalonia. Mum has a worried look on her face. Is she afraid at seeing Yannis after all these years? I know she stopped writing to Yannis and her Mother when Father died. She could not cope with their demands. I recall some talk of the elderly mother planning to come and live with us. We barely had enough to feed ourselves, how could we have managed an elderly person and her complex needs?

Does Mother think that Yannis will berate her? I hope not. My mother and her mother had a difficult relationship. From what I heard, it sounded like her mother was harsh to her. I understand the old lady lived with Yannis and his wife until she died.

I wonder if I have done the wrong thing organising this trip to Cephalonia?

Ring Cath in Australia from the airport; she is home from Taekwondo. She tells me that Dave is fine, has a new girlfriend. Cath finished her exams and passed.

I miss them.

CHAPTER 37

Returning to Athens

Athens

June 1993

Yesterday, Yannis was at the airport to meet us. He was a short man holding a hat, looking as anxious as a bridegroom. It was an emotional welcome. I spotted him first. He looked like a male version of Mother.

"Are you Yannis?" I asked in Greek.

"Yes," he said. He rushed up to Mother with outstretched arms and hugged her.

"My dear sister Ekaterini..." he started crying, overcome with emotion.

I snapped photo after photo. Alan and I cried. Not Mother.

Yannis and Georgina live in a small, colourful home bursting with yellow and orange flowers in clay pots. Yannis old and frail, walks with difficulty, has a walking stick. His wife Georgina, bright and busy, talks nonstop.

Georgina tells me their only child, a precious son born to older parents, died at nineteen years when he tried to break up a fight in a taverna. He was punched, crashed to the ground, and bled to death. The offender jailed for twelve months. I am moved; it is tragic.

Yannis has somehow obtained early photos of our family in Australia. A Greek family who lived in Australia sent him photos of our family. I remember Jim dated a Greek girl. We used to see them a lot. The two mothers were friends, the families shared picnics. We lost contact when the family returned to Greece.

In Australia, the oral history I heard from Mother is that her Mother's name was Polikesina, her father Procopos. Ekaterini was the eldest, then a boy George, followed by twin boys Yannis and Dimitri. Mother said she was taken out of school to help care for the twins. This upset her as she loved school. She wanted to be a dressmaker and begged her father into letting her have sewing lessons. Her mother disapproved.

Mother had been closer to the other twin Dimitri who died from wounds from the war. The older brother George died in her arms, of pneumonia. Yannis was her least favourite brother because her Mother's Polikesina spoiled him.

~

Georgina prepared an aromatic meal of roast lamb, vegetables, and salad. This was followed by big slabs of watermelon. Neighbours come to meet us. We were a curiosity. After the meal, we sat in the cool garden near the vines and talked until midnight.

Yannis and Georgina gave us their bedroom. Mother had the spare room. They insisted on sleeping in the lounge. I felt guilty that they were using the hard divan as they were much older than us. But they would have it no other way.

Mother was chatty and made conversation, Alan friendly and expansive. I felt excited like a child at Christmas.

~

In the morning, breakfast was a treat of pancakes and honey. Yannis used to be a chef on a ship and although he does not cook now, he instructs Georgina what to buy and prepare.

There was a knock on the door. The taxi driver who collected us from the airport arrived to show us the island. We crowded into the taxi and taken on a tour of places of interest around Argostoli. I learnt that Cephalonia lies east of a major tectonic fault, similar to the San Andreas Fault. There are regular earthquakes along this fault. Important natural features include Melissani lake, the Drogarati caves and Koutavos Lagoon in Argostoli. The biggest town on the island is Argostoli. It was totally ruined by earthquakes in 1953 and been rebuilt.

We explored the beautiful cave lake of Melissani; during the day when the sun is high and sunshine falls on the lake makes the blue waters shimmer. We visited magnificent beaches.

More friends and neighbours arrived on our return to the house. Mother again, a minor celebrity.

And surprising, for I never knew my father Michael was a good friend of Yannis. *Who would have thought that my family stretches so far? Yannis speaks well of my father.*

Many stories are shared, Mother's childhood, of growing up in difficult times, of World War II. I have never heard these stories.

I wondered if Mother's coolness to her brother is part of her mental problems? A grudge or something horrible that happened she could not forgive?

Aunt Georgina took me aside and made me promise to bring Mother back next year and stay for a month.

"Please bring her back so Yannis can spend more time together. He has been so happy finding your mother. It would be a tragedy if he never saw her again," she said.

I promised but had no idea how I would manage the trip.

In the late afternoon, we left for the airport and boarded the plane.

I was annoyed and disappointed with Mother. Yannis and his wife Georgina were miserable to see us leave. They were in tears and visibly upset. Mother her head tilted up, did not evoke any emotion, was cold as ice.

"Don't you care about him? He is your only living relative," I said.

She tries to fob me off.

"You should have written to your Mother and brother all those years," I said.

She becomes defensive and said, "Don't spoil things."

~

When our plane landed in Athens, the temperature had soared above forty degrees Celsius. It was so hot, many people have suffered heat stroke and taken by ambulance to the hospital.

We hired a taxi to Taci's, but the traffic snarled up. Taci, his brother, and the two dogs were at Taci's house in the oppressive heat.

No one opens a window or curtain for fresh air to come in. It is darker than ever and more forbidding. But it is Taci's home and he can have it any way he wants.

I am appreciative he is letting us stay with him.

Taci had been drinking, was belligerent again.

Mother and Alan could barely keep their eyes open. Taci demanded we go out with him.

The last thing I need is a repeat of his dangerous drunken driving episode.

So as kindly and as sweetly as I could, I used Mother as an excuse.

He agreed.

We scoffed the delicious cheese puffs that Georgina had cooked and packed for us.

A few hours later Taci returned. He was maudlin, decided to go through the photo albums again and show me photos of his dead wife. He cried at each one.

The dogs continued to menace, the air conditioner rattled. Mother was distant, in her own world. Alan tired and cranky. I headed them to bed.

A little later Taci proposed I go out with him.

"I can't leave Mother in case she needs the toilet."

He accepted this.

In his absence, pack our bags for the cruise tomorrow.

About 11 p.m., Taci comes crashing in. Heard him mumbling and crying. Then silence as he falls on the divan.

~

In the morning, Taci was his usual delightful self, respectful, helpful.

"I have a large snake," he said.

My eyes widen,

"Here?"

"No, on my country property. It lives inside my home for protection," he said.

"Would you like to come and stay at my country place and see the snake?"

I thought about it, a long, terrifying drive with Taci to go to a house with a large snake. As generous as the offer may have been, I declined.

~

We thanked Taci many times for his hospitality and generosity. Showered him with gifts.

Taci is a wonderful conflicted man, so full of love and tenderness and self-destructive.

I love him dearly.

CHAPTER 38

MTS Odysseus

Mediterranean

June 1993

The taxi toots, we are off to Piraeus and the cruise. Mother is exhilarated, eager as a child. I have seen enough mood swings from Mother in the last few weeks to be dizzy.

We pass through customs. I assist Mother up the steel gangplank to the ship.

"Welcome to *Odysseus*," said the boat crew member, and takes us to our rooms.

Our bags are already there. Mother's room is adjoining ours. The cabins comfortable, a round porthole to admire the ocean, bath towels in a pattern on the bed.

Every passenger is directed to the conference room for the safety drill. The room fills with passengers wearing orange safety vests. We are told the safety drill is important, but no one takes it seriously; everyone messes around and makes jokes. Have a glorious photo of Mother laughing; an orange safety vest tied to her chest.

There is a long queue for the buffet lunch. The

passengers are a mixed group. Many are Europeans, Americans, and British. They are a variety of ages, from teenagers to elderly. Some are well-heeled, familiar with cruising. There are Northern European men and women, the women skinny, blonde, and stunning.

The ship is spacious, clean, has several white decks, restaurants, movie theatre, gym, gambling room, dance room, lecture room, gift shops. A city on a boat.

Mother has a snooze. Her snoring resonates through the wall to our cabin and makes Alan and I laugh. She wakes refreshed and overjoyed to be part of the cruise.

"What are we doing next?" she asks.

In the meanwhile, Alan morphs into a green-eyed monster right in front of my eyes. Is jealous and makes nasty remarks if I tend or care for Mother. He perfects his old boorish routine.

Must everyone have to have a turn at being idiotic?

Mother and I make plans to stay and watch the evening floor show.

"I don't want to watch the floor show," Alan said.

"But we do," I said. "You can join us."

"I'm tired," he said. "Come to bed," he yells, people turn to look at us.

I stand my ground and insist that Mother and I wish to watch the promised glittering floor show.

He leaves in a huff.

Mother and I find front seats for the floor show.

It is pure fantasy, sequined dancers spin this way and that, thumping music makes me want to dance with the others. The disco ball glitters and spins above the dancers. The cabaret room twinkles and shines with fairy lights. The audience claps and cheers.

A stunning woman with long, brown hair and trailing sparkly dress split to the thigh sings sad torch songs.

"Why did you leave me when I loved you so..." she croons.

Zorba music erupts, the dance floor becomes alive, men and women holding hands and kicking their feet. We join in and kick and say, "Oopa" with the others. It is a joy to be with happy people who want to have a good time.

After the show, Mother and I tour the boat. The full moon reflected on the water. Young romantics snuggle together, make promises of love. The sea breeze wraps around us. We stretch out on the deck chairs and think of dolphins and fish swimming underneath. It is magical. The stars in the clear sky create a canopy of light above us.

The next day I wake before 6 a.m. eager to embrace the day. Alan and Mother sleep on. I stride briskly to the Jupiter deck of the *Odysseus*. There is only one word for the view—it is *glorious*. Soft light seeps over the sky, bathes the wave tops in a golden hue, a type of yellow wash, a sacred time. The boat has a comforting rhythm. It reminds me of gentle lullabies mothers sing to their babies. The waves fluff against the side of the boat. Small flags flutter on deck.

There are other early birds like me, couples huddle under blankets. I stretch catlike on a white deck chair; it has a bright yellow seat cover.

The waiter brings me an aromatic cup of coffee. This is bliss. Cannot believe my good fortune to be here and to be on a boat travelling to Egypt.

Do sailors ever get bored by the sea's magnificence? I am in love with the sea and the sky and the world. Inhale it deep inside me. Later when I am back in Australia I want to be able to release this image and hold this peaceful moment close. Stamp it inside of me.

Alan is his nice self again.

Breakfast is huge, so many choices; cereal, yogurt, toast, tea coffee, pancakes, bacon, scrambled eggs, poached eggs, boiled eggs. We eat our fill.

The oncoming tour includes Cairo, Jerusalem, and Cyprus. Lectures and slides about Egypt and Israel are shown in the main room.

The Pyramids...I will see the pyramids. Can this be true?

Alan and Mother and I lay on deckchairs and sip tea, watch the horizon. The expanse of water stretches beyond us and merges with the endless blue sky.

"Dolphins," shouts someone.

We rush to the railing. A pod of dolphins swims near the boat.

A person can be as busy or as lazy as they like on board ship.

The Northern Europeans passengers sunbathe nude in hidden areas of the boat. It is no secret. Everyone knows where they sunbathe but are left alone. They crave the sun. Search for it until they are brown and fabulous. The English start off lily white, turn pink and burn. Dark-haired Europeans care less about the sun. It is a United Nations boat, all nationalities. My ears prick up when I hear an Australian accent.

"Where are you from?" asked a woman with an Aussie accent.

"We are from Perth," answered someone else.

Rich-looking Americans smoke thick cigars, blonde wives swagger in white pedal pushers and high heels. Dark European men with dark glasses like a Mafia bosses stroll past. The Greek crew seem to be everywhere, bundles of energy and enjoy a chat.

"How are you enjoying the cruise so far?" A crew member said.

"Have a look on the other side of the ship; you will see flying fish."

The ship offers a variety of activities for the energetic. Ping Pong, Shuffleboard, Blackjack, Trivial Pursuit, Backgammon, and Greek dancing lessons, Treasure hunts, and introduction to gemstones and more. The gift shop is open, as is the gaming room, movie theatres, and swimming pools.

There is always food; snacks, meals, something for everyone.

And of course, there is the wondrous sea.

I notice a sign 'Medical Conference in the Stateroom.' I am curious. The room has thirty American surgeons seated around an instructor as he talks his way through a PowerPoint on cardiac surgery. This must be a dream conference; a few hours of lectures and the rest of the day to enjoy the wonderful cruise, and tax deductable. All winners here.

CHAPTER 39

Excursion to Cairo

Egypt

June 1993

Each tour from the cruise boat is an exercise in strict time-tabling. Some avoid the rush, relax and stay on the boat all day. But those like us who plan to disembark must wake very early. I wake at 4:30 a.m., organise myself and then Mother, have an early breakfast. Our cruise boat arrives at Post Said at 6 a.m. A team of Immigration authorities boards the ship, checks our documents. Each passenger on the tour must carry a passport and Egyptian landing card.

At 7:30 a.m. we disembark for Cairo, step down the steep gangplank, holding fast to Mother and climb into the waiting buses.

The port heaves with people, buses, trucks, cars; they appear to be all tooting and honking. Heavy machinery lifts crates over our heads. The noise deafening.

"Our buses are over there," I shout to Alan, pointing to a group of buses.

I notice that there is one bus in front of our

convoy that has soldiers holding rifles. The same at the back, more armed men clutching rifles. The passengers cram into the middle buses.

"Several tourists were blown up and killed a few months back. It is mandatory to have armed guards to protect tourists," one passenger whispered to me.

I did not know this; we are isolated in Australia, rarely hear of such news. Decide not to tell Mother, she has enough fears. I feel a little shaken, the carefree holiday emotion is gone, replaced with fear and trepidation.

The buses depart in a convoy for the journey to Cairo, Africa's largest city. We use the Desert Road which is heavily congested. The tour guide tells us people are so poor they live on top of graves in the cemetery, called the City of the Dead.

Our buses join hundreds of other buses which disembark at the Museum of Egyptian Antiquities. It is one of the world's most important collections of Ancient Egyptian relics. The museum is stocked with priceless artefacts, gold treasures that are walled behind thick security glass. We gawk at the Pharaoh's treasure and imagine a life where the opulence was paraded as a right of the leaders. And at the same time pushed and shoved from all sides by masses of people craning for a better look.

"Make sure you hold your bags very close to you. Pickpockets and thieves work in this area. Tourists are their target," said the tour guide.

I hang onto Mother so she doesn't get lost. Alan

stays close to us. At the appointed time, the whistle blows, and our tour guide directs us back to our buses.

Next is the Citadel and Alabaster Mosque, both stunning and has great religious significance. Blue lamps hang from the ceiling.

The mosque must be fantastic when it is full of people praying.

"Women must cover their shoulders, arms, and legs," said the guide.

One German tourist refuses to drape a skirt provided to cover her bare legs. She wears tiny red shorts that just cover her buttocks and is refused entry into the Mosque. Later, she enters the mosque wearing a sulky face and the skirt tied over her legs.

Then Giza and lunch at Mena House Oberoi Hotel. It was originally built as a royal hunting lodge for Khedive Ismail. The palace luxurious with magnificent blue and white ceramics and historic paintings.

Next the Pyramids and Sphinx, built as massive tombs on the order of the Pharaohs more than 4,000 years ago. They were constructed by the back-breaking strength of thousands of slave workers. The massive blocks of rock defy how they could have been moved from one place to here and then stacked individually on top of each other to make the pyramid. We are denied entrance into the Pyramids for safety reasons,

Swarms of persistent traders demand we buy postcards and cheap trinkets.

"Do not buy from these sellers; they use tricks to pick your pocket and steal your watch while they sell you postcards," the guide said earlier.

We shake our heads and say no to the sellers, but they circle us like locusts.

The Sphinx is a sentinel to history. I saw *Ben Hur* when I was young and have been mesmerised with all things Egyptian ever since. The city sits on the edge of the Sphinx which has the body of a lion, a symbol of kingship representing might. The human head symbolises intelligence. The Sphinx faces east where it can observe the rising sun, the return of life. Its nose is broken. I wonder how many rising suns it has witnessed. Egypt is a haunting country.

It is hot, wet patches appear on under arms and around necks. Mercifully the bus is air-conditioned, a relief to step into the cool.

Fun camel rides are available for the brave. It does not look like fun to me, especially when the camels bolted, and the riders screamed in panic.

We buy Cartouches for the family; they resemble oblong gold with names written in Hieroglyphics.

Mother slips and falls badly getting off the bus. She is not hurt but shaken and has grazed her leg.

"Do you want to stay on the bus in the cool?" I asked.

"No," she said, emphatic and clear.

The trip must challenge her comfort zone.

Mother dozes on the bus when we drive from one place to another.

"Did you see this or that?" Alan and I ask each other.

The buses disembark at the Papyrus Institute and Bazaar. We buy papyrus gifts and journey to Cairo and Ismailia to Port Said.

Are back on board by 8 p.m., overexcited and overstimulated. Pinch ourselves at the good fortune to see so much, eat a light meal.

Later, when the others are in bed, I lay on the deckchair and consider the black ocean. Try to remember history lessons from school about Egypt. Which Pharaoh did what, who were the brilliant mathematicians and astronomers.

I cannot believe my good fortune to have had a brief glimpse of Egypt.

CHAPTER 40

Jerusalem

Israel

June 1993

Again, up at the crack of dawn, breakfast, passports, security passes. Travel down the gang plank; holding Mother and our things and into Israel.

The young tour guide is Jewish. He is friendly, tells jokes, and tall tales, keeps us amused. I notice every corner has soldiers in uniform; they carry large rifles, even the women carry huge military weapons. Security is tight; bags are repeatedly inspected.

I shiver, realise we are in a world conflict zone, one of the most dangerous places on earth.

~

The bus takes us to Jerusalem, a holy city for three religions; Christianity, Judaism, and Islam. Crowds jostle and pray and stare at the historical buildings. Our guide speaks about each religion in turn and its section of Jerusalem. There is overlap, certain areas claimed by all three religions. Each square inch of the place cries out history and is sacred.

No wonder the area this is a conflict zone.

We visit The Church of the Holy Sepulchre; multiple lamps hang from the ceiling. Crowds jam in the doorway to see.

"This is where Jesus was born," said the guide.

A glass partition covers the area on the floor, underneath the stable where Mary gave birth. The Church of the Nativity built by Emperor Justinian on the site of the stall where Jesus was born.

Mother crawls on hands and knees and kisses the glass.

"This is where Jesus' body was placed after he was brought down from the cross," the guide points to a large square of thick stone with overhanging lamps.

"God bless us," said Mother.

Mother is in her element. She cries, kisses the stone, crosses herself, over and over, lights candles. Looks upward, she is in religious rapture and high on emotion, tears run down her face. I hold her arm. Steady her. She is oblivious to me. Is in another space and time. In a trance, a look of pure joy on her face. The flickering candles create an out of body experience. Alan looks on, bemused.

"Watch out for pickpockets," he whispers in my ear. "That young chap is staying too close to you."

I look around and peer at the young boy who has

edged close to Mother who is oblivious to the world around her.

"I'll hold your bag," I said, taking her bag.

Not that it has anything of value in it—sunglasses a hankie, small amount of money. The young boy slinks off.

The guide moves us on. Mother continues in her rapture at every site, kisses everything of religious significance. It is not easy for her as there many steps to navigate, never complains, takes it in her stride.

Young boys hassle us to buy trinkets. I buy a handful of wooden crosses for gifts.

The guide cautions us to stay together, not to wander off from the group. Two tourists were stabbed the other day. A stranger ran a knife into pilgrims praying.

We bunch up close. And tread the walk, Via Dolososa, that Jesus took dragging his cross. The area cobbled stoned and narrow in parts. We envisage how it would have been for Jesus, crown of thorns on his head and dragging a huge wooden cross across the cobblestones. The guide points to the area when a stranger came to Jesus' aide when he was about to faint from exhaustion. History is replaying in front of us. Jerusalem transforms people who are true believers. Are gripped with the veracity of Biblical stories and are living the experiences.

"I can't believe I am really here," Mother repeats, crossing herself.

She is glowing, has a light from inside.

"I have touched the stone that Jesus touched. I walked the walk of Jesus carrying his cross. I am blessed." She pauses to take breathe.

"Thank you, God."

She opens her arms to Alan and me, holds us tight.

"I am so happy; thank you Alan and Cally."

We are too emotional to speak.

A baby born in a stable, his family refugees, born 2,000 years still can transform lives in the twentieth century.

We pass the Roman Foundation, through the Bazaar and to the Western Wall. The Wall built 2,000 years is the most holy of all Jewish sites. The Wall is known as the Wailing Wall; people pray and leave notes.

Lunch is at the Ramat Rachael Hotel.

Return to the boat at 5 p.m. Mother and Alan rest; I am too euphoric to go to sleep. Walk around the cruise ship, hang over the rails searching for dolphins, sit on a deck chair, and stare at the moving and everchanging sea. Think deep thoughts about life and death and the significance of being.

CHAPTER 41

Limassol

Cyprus

June 1993

The boat cruise has been a fabulous dream come true. But I had no idea how tiring the tours are for old and young alike. It has taken a toll on us, we are exhausted, Mother fading, Alan snippy. I am bewildered as to time and space and too much togetherness, too much activity and stimulation. There is so much to experience and see. And I want to see it all for I know will never again have another opportunity. There is a manic pace about fitting everything in.

"Happy birthday, Alan," Mother and I chirp.

"Oh, you remembered," he said and opened the parcels.

In the morning, the usual rush, arrive in Limassol, Cyprus. Disembark for the tour to Paphus, passports, documents, landing tags, down gangplanks, in buses, out of buses, rush and rush.

The bus takes us through Cyprus, Turkish and Greek camps at opposite ends of the island. Greeks make up eighty percent of the population, mostly army, the rest Turkish. Paphos is a city on the southwest coast and has several sites relating to the cult of goddess Aphrodite. It is said her mythical birthplace was at Old Paphos. Aphrodite's Rock where, reputedly, the goddess emerged from the sea.

New Paphos has an impressive modern harbor, ancient ruins, fortresses, and villas at the Archaeological Park. The bus stops at the famous House of Dionysus, which is preserved under cover.

"This is an extraordinary example of a Roman House of the third century AD," said the guide.

The house is arranged around a classical atrium, with brightly coloured mosaic floors depicting Roman legends.

The colour and intricacies of the mosaics clear and bight. I try to visualise the Roman home with slaves and grandeur.

Mother is awkward and stiff, and becoming a dead weight to move up and down stairs and steps. Although she finds it difficult to get around, astonishes me with her interest and is excited about whatever we are doing.

Later the three of us chill out on the deck after the tour, sipping cold frappe, watching the magnificent ocean and the world go by.

"I am having a wonderful time," Mother said. "But I loved Jerusalem best."

"The pyramids were the best for me," said Alan.

I loved everything.

A special Greek Taverna Dinner has been organised on board. Greek food, Greek dancing. Perfect. A handsome Captain in full dress uniform, white jacket and pants, gold trim sits at our table. He is intrigued we are Australians.

"You are very far away from home," he said. He makes light conversation and moves to the next table.

CHAPTER 42

Kusadasi-Ephesus and Patmos

The final day on the cruise

July 1993

Mother is adamant she will not step on Turkish soil when the boat stops at Kusadasi. She stays behind on the boat. I shower, dress, give eye drops, and medicine and arrange one of the staff to keep an eye on her and bring breakfast to her room.

At 6:30 a.m., we disembark in Turkey. Alan and I enjoy the exhilarating morning. Little green frogs hop in front of us. My reading of Ephesus suggested an extensive history and culture. It was founded by Leleges people in 3000 B.C. Many civilizations, including Roman Empire, Christianity, and Turkish have a history in the region. Saint John the Evangelist and the Virgin Mary lived in Ephesus at one stage.

The city is built of marble. Hadrian's library, The Agor and the city's Bordello are some of the many buildings still standing. The amphitheatre faces the ancient harbour and can seat many. Apostle Paul preached here and told the crowds there was only one God. The guide informs us there was an underground tunnel linking the library to the Bordello opposite.

Back on the boat by 11:30 a.m. Mother had a peaceful day and was well looked after by the crew.

We sail for Patmos, a small island in the Dodecanese group (twelve islands) that has played a significant role in Biblical history. The grotto has a tiny cave where John the Divine wrote the book of Revelations aided by an angel.

The Fortress Monastery built atop a hill dates from the eleventh century. It houses astonishing Byzantine Bibles kept under secure glass.

"I want to see the room where Saint John wrote the book of Revelation," said Mother.

"It is steep," I said.

She will not be persuaded otherwise.

Alan and I half-carry her down the steps to the room where St John wrote the Book of Revelations.

"Oh my God," said Mother, crossing herself, kneeling, kissing the ground.

The room has a sacred feel. I close my eyes and try to capture an image of an old man with a quilt pen writing on parched skin canvas, a shining angel at his side.

~

Back on the boat, we wear our best clothes for the formal dress-up dinner. Many of the passengers wear elegant, long gowns and fur stoles. Some partners dressed in white dinner jackets and bow ties. The meal has a festive feel to it.

The next day we arrive in Piraeus, disembark. Wait an hour for our bags to be unloaded. Shambles of the highest order. Piraeus is chocked with people and cars.

By a stroke of good fortune, commandeer a taxi.

Most of the affordable Athens hotels have been booked out. But we locate one that is cheap and cheerful. We were too tired to care.

CHAPTER 43

Dionia Hotel

Athens

July 1993

We are hot and bothered, soaked in sweat and perspiration. Our faces red. The heat makes us dizzy and bad-tempered. Hotel Dionia is not cool, despite the air conditioner blasting my ears like a Mack truck. But cooler than outside where it is sweltering, forty something degrees in Athens.

Mother is unwell; her legs hurt. It is difficult to get a word of communication out of her, is beyond tired.

Alan is hot and cross; we squabble about the room. I decide to pay for an extra day for Mother's room so she can rest comfortably until it is time to depart to the airport at 8 p.m. I did not want her sitting for hours in the waiting room in this hot, cheap hotel.

We all park in her room. Mother stretched on the single bed, we in the chairs.

It is too hot to go outside.

CHAPTER 44

Returning home

Athens

July 1993

We arrive at the Athens airport at 8 p.m., wait for clearance to go through customs. The departure lounge is old and shabby. The toilets don't work. I must go through security, down two floors, and walk a while to find a toilet. I know this because I have just made the distance with Mother.

I attempt to ring Taci and Renulla, but they are both out.

At the allocated time, we present our tickets, go through security. Am thrilled to discover that the departure tax has already been paid in Australia. It was on the tickets, but I cannot read Greek. What a blessing. We are jubilant.

We use the money I have put aside for the departure tax for a final delicious Greek meal of roast lamb and potatoes.

Board the plane at midnight. Alan and Mother are asleep before take-off.

I try to sleep but can't. The twenty-three-hour

flight felt like a prison sentence. But survive and make it home.

Take Mother back, sort her things, put her to bed.

She has been marvellous.

It has been a wonderful trip, once in a lifetime.

I am amazed at the things we accomplished. The people we connected with; Renulla, Taci and families, Yannis and Georgina. The cruise, something I never expected.

We survived in one piece. No illness. No problems.

How lucky we are.

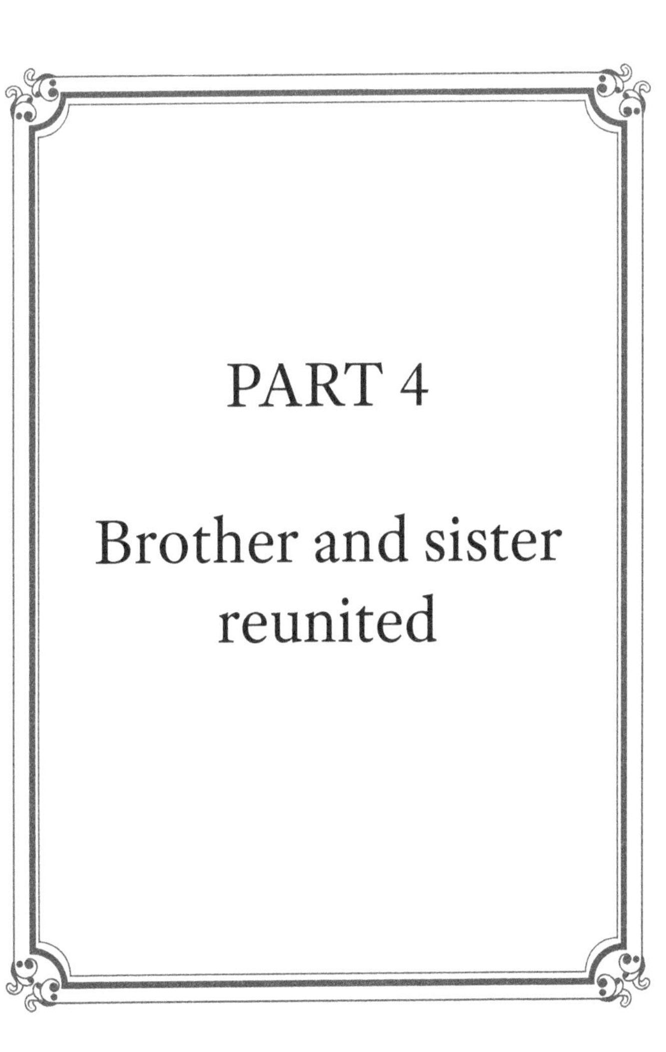

PART 4

Brother and sister reunited

CHAPTER 45

Brother and sister reunited

Cephalonia

June 1994

Last year, I promised Mother and Yannis that we would return to Cephalonia. I am aware that time running out for both. They are old, and who knows how long they will live. Last year, Mother, Alan, and I saw a little of Cephalonia. This year Yannis and Georgina asked us to stay a few weeks with them.

Cephalonia is in an earthquake zone; many minor earthquakes occur each year. In 1953, a massive earthquake caused mass destruction destroying the island and killing many. Now rebuilt and popular with tourists, especially from England. Is blazing hot in summer, we will be there in summer.

During World War II, Cephalonia was occupied by Italian and German forces. I have read the novel *Captain Corelli's Mandolin* by the English author Louis de Bernieres who was inspired by the occupation. I had romantic notions of the island and its inhabitants. Have read the travel brochures about the island, eager to explore Lixouri, Fiscardo, Assos, and Kourkoumelata. Hope to visit the beautiful cave lake of Melissani again. Another on my list of places to see is the Agios Gerasimos Monastery. Saint Gerasimos died in 1579, has the honour of being the patron saint of the island.

My friends are envious of me travelling to the Greek islands.

"Can I come with you? I will carry your bags," they joke.

Uncle Yannis and Aunt Georgina live in Argostoli, the main town, they insist we stay with them. I would have preferred to stay in a hotel.

"Have you bought the wool cardigans for Yannis and Georgina?" said Mother.

"They are packed in my suitcase," I tell her.

It is cold in winter in the islands.

I purchase smaller gifts such as tea towels with cheerful motifs, small furry koalas, and picture books describing Australia. Wash and pack the clothes, sort out the passports, money.

Mother and I have talked of nothing else for months; she is pleased to see Uncle Yannis and Aunt Georgina, or so she tells me.

On the day of our departure, Alan drives us to the airport.

"Have a great time," he said.

"I wish I could go with you. Give my best wishes to Georgina and Yannis."

Mother is dressed in her best blue dress, a wide smile on her face. She has her favourite blue-and-white scarf around her neck. I wear my good black trouser suit and white shirt, my travelling staple.

There are long queues at the check-in. And the rubbery smell of sneakers, body sweat, and tobacco breath. Groups of excited men and women and children line at the counters.

"Where are my medicines and eye drops?" said Mother.

"Here," I said, holding up the carry-on luggage bag."

Our bags are weighed, placed on the conveyor belt to the plane.

I have never flown Gulf Air before and chose this airline because of the cheap tickets that were offered to entice passengers to their new service operating out of Melbourne. I catch a whiff of floral perfume as the Gulf Air flight attendants pass. They wear a jaunty scarf draped over pillbox caps and around their necks and are exotic. The male attendants walking behind wear smart, striped jackets.

We slip through the customs door, passports stamped, paperwork in order. We scan the duty-free shops, so many tempting and glittery. Perfume of every type is on sale. We experiment with the expensive ones. I like "Joy" perfume best with its lingering flower essence.

"Mmmm lovely," I said. "The perfume reminds me of grand houses and old money."

We don't buy anything. The aroma of freshly brewed coffee tempts us, and we sip coffee and eat a sugary bun. Approach the departure lounge, brimming with noisy Greeks who are on a tour. They crack jokes, laugh, and fool around. A happy crowd, intent on having a wonderful time. Their enthusiasm affects us and we laugh with them.

"There will be a short delay in take-off," said the ground attendant at the departure lounge.

"How long?" one woman asked.

"Not sure," said the attendant, shrugging her shoulders.

I should have known something was amiss when our departure was delayed the second and third time. When sandwiches and blankets were handed out by the ground staff, I knew the delay was suspicious.

"What's going on?" asked Mother, face wrinkled with concern.

"A delay of sorts," I said.

We curl under the white blankets and doze. The departure lounge resembles a hostel for the homeless. After midnight, the passengers are bussed to the hotel opposite the airport to stay overnight. The official version listed as 'mechanical problems.'

This is an omen. I could have cancelled the trip and returned home. But as usual, I was too full of romantic notions of a loving reunion of brother and sister.

The next day a bus collected us from the hotel, again passed through customs and finally we board. The plane has been recently cleaned and smelt of disinfectant. Everything appeared to be in order. The flight attendants stood in the aisles and enthusiastically recited the safety drill waving their arms this way and that informed emergency exits. The Greek group does not listen but chattered amongst themselves. One man burst into a Greek song and the others joined in.

Mother grinned, "I feel I am in Greece already," she said.

The engines roared, obliterated conversations, we vibrated with the plane as it hurtled down the runway. Once airborne, the Greek passengers erupted into wolf whistles and applause. Notice most of the plane seats are taken by the group. They are already in holiday mood. When the seatbelt sign goes off, the Greek group clog the aisles as they moved around in conversation.

"Hey Kostas, not long now...when we are in Athens I will beat you to the Parthenon," a man said.

"You are too old for the steep hill; I will be there before you," the other man said.

"Let's make a wager..." said the first man, slapping the second man on the back.

Four hours into the flight, the captain speaks over the public-address system.

"Excuse me ladies and gentlemen. Unfortunately, we will be disembarking in Bahrain. You will be taken to the Gulf Air Hotel until the small mechanical problem with the plane is fixed."

A loud groan comes from the passengers, followed by unpleasant mutterings.

I feel uneasy; is the plane unsafe?

"Are we landing in Athens?" asks Mother.

I try to explain and realise she doesn't understand.

Running through my mind is the fear of losing our booking at the Stanley Hotel in Athens. It is the high tourist season and the room booked several weeks in advance.

"Calel," Mother said.

"When we are in Cephalonia I want to visit Saint Gerasimos Monastery. My grandmother told me stories about Saint Gerasimos and how he cured people of mental illnesses."

"Yes, of course," I said, wondered what she was thinking.

The plane lands in Bahrain in the afternoon. We are ushered through customs as a tight group, climb into buses that ferry us directly to the Gulf Hotel.

I am thrilled at this turn of events as I have never been to Bahrain.

A hotel staff member ushers us to our small drab room.

"I want to have a sleep," Mother said.

Settle Mother to bed.

Take the opportunity while she sleeps to see a little of Bahrain. To me, it symbolises something exotic. An Aladdin's lamp of magic.

I order tea and make myself comfortable in the hotel lobby, am an observer of the world of Bahrain. Tall, dark-skinned men move through, wearing a variety of headgear. Some have loose cloths held at the crown by coloured rope; some wear turbans. They wear white, flowing gowns and appear to dominate the landscape and speak in Arabic and clipped English. They seem to be on a mission and appear to flow through the hotel. Their women follow several steps behind, clothed in black, floor-length burkas that cover face and body. I read an article that suggested that underneath the restrictive burkas, these women are clothed in designer clothes and priceless jewels.

The hotel lobby is luxurious, opulent, and marble on every surface. There are a number of colourful comfortable sofas placed in strategic waiting points. An enormous shaft of water cascades from above into a tiled pool, gives off coolness. The sound of the water soft as a mother's lullaby. It is a fantasy place tucked away from the dense heat and oppressive conditions out in the street.

Four English tourists are engrossed in a soccer match on the wide television screen. The men erupt into wild shouts whenever a player kicks a goal.

In another section of the vast foyer, sit a group of uniformed female Gulf Air flight attendants. I move closer towards the group, pretending to flip through a magazine. The attendants speak English with American, English, and Philippine accents. They are movie star gorgeous—blonde, brunette and black-haired, immaculately made up and groomed. They look like beautiful dolls.

"I was recruited in London," said one to a friend.

"New York for me," another attendant said.

I notice the textbook they are studying, 'ditching drills.' Hope they learn that part well; if we ditch at sea, I want more than beauty from these women.

Our flight group is instructed to be at reception desk just after midnight. The luxurious foyer is packed with passengers and their suitcases. We bunch around the marble counter, impatient for our passports.

The manager, a small, dark man with a thin black moustache, coughs three times. He turns his head one way and then another before staring at us.

The group falls silent.

"Someone..." he stops for emphasis.

"Someone in this group has taken the little bottles of alcohol from their room. Will that person return the bottles or pay for them?"

No one moves.

After a time, he speaks in a slow, deliberate voice. "We have your passports...."

The emphasis is on passports, allows it to sink in.

"No passports will be given out until the alcohol is paid for or returned," he said.

The passengers stare at the manager.

"Oh, my God," said one woman, puts her hand to her mouth. "We will be stuck in this country."

"Whoever has not paid for the bottles, do it now," said a tall Greek man from the group.

Loud voices erupt; men and woman shout, others throw their hands in the air. Everyone knows the consequences of being without a passport. People point to each other.

"Was it you?"

They have become a pack of dogs snarling and snapping at each other.

Mother's eyes wide in terror.

I try to keep calm.

The manager rocks on his feet.

Eventually, a middle-aged Greek woman, red-faced with embarrassment, opens a large handbag and places several miniature liqueur bottles on the marble counter. They resemble tiny babies in a row.

"I thought they were free," she said in a small voice.

"Good, very good," said the manager, nods his head several times.

The group burst into condemnation of the manager.

"Such a lot of fuss for such small bottles," said a thin woman.

"Now you can have your passports," the manager said.

"The bus is waiting outside to take you to the airport." He points to the door.

We collect our passports and scramble to the buses.

~

The terminal is crowded. In one area, twenty Indian women in red, yellow, and orange saris are spread out on seats. Some sleep. A few women with expressionless eyes glance at the passing human traffic. The women are strangely silent. Notice fear in one young girl's brown face creased with apprehension. They are foreign workers contracted into Bahrain to work for the locals. They are often mistreated by their masters I am told.

A steel wheelchair is provided for Mother and we are whisked through customs and are the first to arrive on the plane. Sometime later, the Greek group streams onto the plane. They silently find their seats and buckle up. No one laughs or jokes. I notice the flight attendants on the plane were those studying for their exams.

"We apologise for the delay and hope you have been well looked after," the captain said over the public address.

Displeased mutterings fill the plane.

The plane takes off with no further problems.

Eventually, we land in Istanbul, again disembark. This time for four hours, the airport teems with dark-skinned men and women. There is nothing to do but wait. Mother looks dishevelled and unhappy.

"Are we in Greece?" she asks, hearing a woman converse in Greek.

I don't tell her we are in Turkey, knowing she will panic, as she harbours a deep fear of all things Turkish.

"Soon," I said, "very soon."

We step off the plane in Athens to the usual bedlam. People pour through customs, again the lackadaisical attitude of a few customs officers. As I feared, the Stanley Hotel cancelled our room booking when we were stranded in Bahrain. After much searching, locate a cheap hotel for the night, Athens airport's International Hotel.

A Greek passenger from the tour group, Anastasia, has befriended me; rushes to assist with Mother as I try to hail a taxi holding jetlagged Mother and our luggage. No luck, am ignored. Anastasia takes control and calls a taxi over.

"Take this lady and her Mother to the International Hotel," she said.

"No...no, the journey is too short," he said shaking his head.

Anastasia swears at him, gestures to a policeman.

"You must take these ladies to the hotel," the police officer said.

The driver grumbles, refuses to assist me with the suitcases. At the hotel, I yank the bags out of the boot with one hand, while holding onto Mother with the other. She is so tired she cannot stand up. I pay the driver and offer a tip. He stares at the tip, pulls a face and throws the tip to the ground.

Welcome to Athens.

"Are we in Athens?" Mother said in a small voice.

"Yes, we will stay in Athens tonight and tomorrow we will fly to Cephalonia and be with Yannis and Georgina," I said.

She nods. But I doubt she understands.

Put Mother to bed.

Find a phone, ring Alan.

"We made it to Athens," I said.

"Yannis rang to find out where you are; he fears you are both lost in transit," he said.

I ring Uncle Yannis, explain the plane problems and the delay, promise we will be in Cephalonia tomorrow. That is the plan. I am not sure of anything anymore.

Locate the breakfast room, book transport for the next day. Walk the corridors to improve the circulation to my stiff and swollen legs. The hotel room is simple, hot and stuffy. The rooms need a fresh coat of paint. Planes fly directly overhead as we are on the runway parameter.

Dogs bark in the room next door.

"I need to go to the toilet," Mother said.

She calls me the minute I drift off to sleep.

Next to us, someone takes a shower, the water pipes scream. On the other side of our room, a man shouts abuse, bangs a door as he leaves, a woman is left behind loudly crying.

~

Morning brings a brighter Mother, but she has the trace of the distant look I fear. Organise breakfast. The taxi connects us to the domestic terminal.

The flight to Cephalonia is without incident.

CHAPTER 46

Cephalonia

1994

Aunt Georgina meets us at the small airport in Cephalonia. She runs to greet us, radiates a warm welcome.

"How are you? How was your flight? Yannis is at home," hugs us both.

"I am so glad you made it. Yannis can talk of nothing else but seeing you again."

The taxi takes us to their home. The purple wisteria cascades over the fence creating a curtain of colour.

A small, stooped, white-haired man holding tight to a walking stick limps out of the front door when he hears the taxi toot.

"Welcome back," Uncle Yannis said holding us both.

"Let me look at you," he said. He holds his hands in a gentle gesture to Mother's face, stares into her eyes.

"Still the same wonderful Ekaterini," and scoops Mother in another gigantic hug.

We are ushered into the cosy kitchen with the red flowered tiles, sit around the table with the white cloth.

"How are you?" he asks Mother.

"I was so worried when you didn't come on the due date." He stops.

"Do you remember when we were children...." He starts a long story about their childhood.

Mother does not say much.

I have permission to tape their conversations and remembrances. Find the stories enjoyable, jot the main points. I never heard these stories. Mother never told me much about her childhood. Yannis paints a happy family, adds bits about the brothers misbehaving. He has had time to dilute the past and make it more pleasurable.

"Do you remember when..." he said over and over to Mother.

Sometimes he laughs.

He is pleased to have a witness to his early life that only Mother can verify. She smiles, nods, is a sounding board for happier times. Now and then she adds a little to the stories. But it is mostly Yannis's story. I feel sorry for him. He smokes, watches television, or is in bed. He cannot venture far from his house except for doctor's appointments. Shuffles painfully, stands up to eat when the leg spasms hit, shakes all the time. I notice he takes a large collection of pain and other medication, including antidepressants.

Uncle Yannis has changed in one year. Is shrunken, bent and frail, relying on the walking stick to get around. Grimaces in pain as he walks. But his joy at being with his sister is evident. Has a cheeky grin, like a boy caught in the act of doing something naughty. Wears a grey sleeveless cardigan over a white shirt.

Aunt Georgina slips on a flowered apron over her dress and prepares Greek coffee cooked over a small gas jet. Next to the coffee cups, a plate of sugared almond biscuits.

"I cooked them this morning," she said.

"What happened to your leg, Yannis?" asked Mother, apprehension written on her face.

"Ahh..." he said.

"I had an operation to my leg, but the stupid surgeon made a mistake and damaged the nerves. Now I am in pain every minute of the day. Nothing can be done but feed me pills for the pain."

"Poor Yannis," said Mother, patting his hand.

"What is worse," said Aunt Georgina. "He also has shingles on his chest and back."

Yannis nods his head.

"Every day is worse than the last."

I begin to feel uncomfortable, wondering if we will complicate an already difficult situation.

Georgina senses my thoughts.

"Yannis has been counting the days until you came." She stands up.

"Can I help?" I said.

"Sit down; talk to Yannis while I serve lunch," she said.

She opens the oven door, the kitchen fills with the delicious aroma of roast goat and vegetables.

The meal is perfect; tender slices of roast goat surrounded by crisp roast potatoes and pumpkin. The meat melts in my mouth, the vegetables crisp.

"Delicious," Mother and I said.

After the meal, snuggle Mother down for a sleep; the journey to Cephalonia has been hard for her.

Locate the local telephone box, ring Alan. I don't want to use Yannis's home phone for international calls so as not to run up their phone bill. Instead, use prepaid phone cards which operate from the numerous public phones.

After my third attempt, I connect with Australia.

"It is all bad news this end. Uncle Jack has died," Alan said. "Aunt Maisie is heartbroken," he stops for a moment. "My mother is having a terrible time with Dad and his Alzheimer's," he said.

We talk for a while.

It appears everyone is having difficulties.

"I will ring in a couple of days," I said.

"Give my love to everyone. Say hello to the children for me."

That evening we eat the remains of the goat. Normally the main meal is lunch and anything left over is reheated for dinner or eaten cold. Again, the meal is perfect, but the serve is too much for me.

Georgina pulls a hurt look when I ask, "Can I have a little less on my plate?"

Eventually bedtime for Yannis and Mother. Uncle Yannis settles in his bedroom to watch the news channel from the small television. Mother sleeps.

Georgina and I make a quick escape to the city square in the evening. It is cooler, the square buzzing with people going back and forth, everyone out for a good time in restaurants and tavernas. Bouzouki music blasts from a taverna, followed by enthusiastic laughing and dancing. The smell of roasted lamb turning on a spit lingers in the air. Long grape vines dangle from shops and eateries.

Young women cling to their partners on screaming motorbikes. No one wears helmets. That hasn't changed.

We are home by 11 p.m.

The heat is stifling in the house. The room where we sleep has permanently closed windows. We are forbidden to open them. A sad air conditioner sits is in the corner but is not used as is too expensive to run. A small fan moves the heat around the room.

Sleep in fragments. Mother's snoring and toilet trips wake me every hour.

~

Each morning the air is cool and still, a promise of a new bright day. Later, the sun beats down, piercing unbearable heat.

After breakfast, Aunt Georgina and I hurry to the market where she hassles with the storekeepers for food at the best price. I carry the cane basket. She buys fresh food daily. The market is crowded.

Pigs' heads hang from iron hooks above my head; the smell of a thousand fish and calamari fills the air.

Uncle Yannis was a chef, now he directs the choice of meals, and supervises Georgina as she prepares and cooks.

When we return home, Aunt Georgina ties the apron around her waist, starts preparing lunch.

"Can I peel the potatoes?" I ask.

"No, you look after your Mother," Aunt Georgina said. "And I will look after everything else."

It does not sound fair, but am a guest in their home, so do not argue.

Sometimes I take Mother out for a short walk to the local church where she lights a candle. If we take too long, Georgina shouts at me as Yannis is waiting anxiously to spend time with her.

Sigh, but say nothing, can feel a closing in.

Mother has her hands continually at her lips and gazes in the distance.

Georgina mentions that Mother stares into space and appears to be talking to herself.

"She is getting old," I said.

"Yannis's mother was the same," said Georgina. "She was like your mother, talked to herself all the time, and blind with glaucoma..." she paused.

"Yannis's mother and I did not get on. She told me many times that I was not the right woman for Yannis."

I ponder on the genetics of schizophrenia and glaucoma.

Each day, Yannis has more of the same stories. Have stopped taping them as they are repeats of the previous day's stories. He relishes his new audience.

Mother looks as though she is in a trance. Every now and then I attempt to change the subject, make small talk, but Yannis is not interested. His brain wired to the far ago school days.

Perhaps he has early dementia.

Each meal is beautifully cooked, delicious, but way too much for me. I am not used to such large servings.

If I leave some on my plate, Georgina is insulted.

"I have spent all day cooking for you, the least you can do is eat it all," said Georgina.

My clothes feel tight and know I have put on weight.

Mother's mental state deteriorates. The psyche medication does not help. She is acting weird. Distracted, again talking to invisible people. There is nothing I can do.

When we are alone, she peers into my face with immense hatred.

"You devil, did you bring me here to kill me? Then will you be satisfied?" She asked through gritted teeth.

Again, in her eyes, I am the poisonous enemy, the persecutor and the cause of all her ills. It is all familiar to me.

I don't understand, am perplexed. Mother wanted to come. The letters back and forth from

Cephalonia begged us to come. She has talked about the trip for months.

"When we are in Cephalonia..." she said.

But now I am the enemy that dragged her here.

Much has changed in a year since we were here last. Uncle Yannis is not the man from last year. The botched operation left him an invalid, racked with unrelenting chronic pain.

Mother has altered as well, is older and easily disorientated. Now picks at her lips until they bleed and mutters under her breathe to the voices.

One day, I excuse myself to fill a prescription for Mother's medication. I find a hidden corner of an alley and cry with frustration.

What to do? Am trapped in a living nightmare. How can I manage this torment?

Should I make an excuse and return to Australia?

On my return, Yannis's screams of pain can be heard from the outside.

"God, kill me," he shouts. "I cannot bear the pain."

Georgina has become snippy with us; she complains that all she does is work. This is true; she never sits still. I offer to help over and over. Try to be of assistance. But she refuses my help. If she catches me clearing the table or stacking the dishes to wash them, she takes personal affront. I am only allowed to dry the dishes but not to put them away.

Feel for Georgina, trapped having to cook and look after us and a sick and demanding husband.

Yannis's cries of pain bring tears to all of us.

Georgina confides she would rather keep busy than think.

"If I think too much I will go crazy," she said dabbing her eyes with the corner of her apron.

"Mother and I are too much work for you," I said.

"No, Yannis is happiest he has been for a long time with you and your Mother here. I wish you could stay longer."

"Perhaps we should leave earlier with Yannis so sick," I said.

"No, no, no...I wish you could change your flights to stay longer," she said.

"I have to return to work," I said.

How could I have got it so wrong? I am so stupid, trying to help two old people be together and it is a disaster. No one is having a good time.

~

"I told you to put the toilet paper in the bin next to the toilet, not flush it in the toilet." Georgina nags me.

I forget every so often. If she finds I have not done that, obviously snooping, she shouts at me.

Apparently, the plumbing is poor and toilet paper clogs the pipes.

~

I have hatched a small plan to save my mind, the little I have left. Early mornings and in the afternoon after lunch when the oldies rest, I plan a short escape.

Sometimes walk to the fisherman's taverna and have a cold frappe by myself. Once took a quick ferry boat trip to another island. A few times made it to the beach and swam.

I have one hour of freedom and plan my time carefully.

This time when I return, neighbours are in the garden with Yannis. Meet the young boy who translates my English letters to Yannis. Have a gift for him, a toy koala. He loves it. The letters are a process. I write in English, and the letter is translated by the young boy. Uncle Yannis and Aunt Georgina write in Greek and my friend Eva translates their letters. Mother has lost the ability to read Greek.

I note Yannis does not talk about the past with the neighbours, a slight change in conversation.

~

Am still nervous speaking Greek. I know I communicate in simple, child-like way. The Greek learnt from oral speech gleaned from my parents. It makes conversation awkward and fuels my stress levels. I do understand much of what is said in Greek but struggle to respond in correct grammar.

Mother is no help when I ask for assistance in finding a Greek word.

"What is bridge in Greek?" I asked.

"Bridge," she said in English. She looks at me as though I am stupid.

"Bridge is English, what is it in Greek?"

"I told you bridge," she said in English.

~

At night when all is quiet; Georgina and I sit next to each other in the kitchen while she watches her beloved Greek soap operas. They are colourful twisted tales of love and betrayal. Like all soap operas, the women have flowing blond hair and men handsome and tall.

When I go to bed it starts, Mother wakes and demands the toilet. Hisses abuse at me.

"You are the devil," she said.

Am dog-tired, do not respond. Mental illness is soul-destroying for the carers.

Where is the lovely happy Mother that came to Lesvos with me? I was the best girl in the world then, now the worst.

A greater force controls her.

She is mentally ill, I tell myself. But it gives me no comfort. Why do the voices have to attack me? I am the one who is good and kind to her.

~

Each morning, rise early, wash Mother's soiled

dresses and underwear, hang them on the clothesline. The clothesline is perched on the flat roof of the house.

Georgina beckons me.

“You have not pegged the clothes properly. All the towels should be together. The underwear has to be inside and the towels on the outside,” she said, wagging a finger at me.

Look at her blankly, about to laugh, then realise she is serious.

“People going past will judge us if the clothes are not hung right,” she said.

I had a mental picture of women in the street clumping together to discuss my pegging skills; suggesting I may be a university lecturer but a failure at pegging.

~

On a festival day of the spirits, Georgina and I visit the cemetery where their son is buried. A neighbour minds Mother and Yannis. The headstone on their beloved son grave is elaborate, a portrait of a lovely young face man surrounded by angelic angels. He died when he was nineteen, twelve years ago. Georgina visits every few weeks.

Yannis and Georgina still mourn him. He was the joy of their lives.

~

The neighbour, Philomena, communicates with Yannis and Georgina through the wide mesh wire that separates the two backyards. There are seats at both sides of the wire. At one spot, the wire opens into a small gate and is a convenient shortcut between the houses. Conversations behind the wire are a daily ritual.

Yannis retells the same stories he told us about the past. The neighbour has a forced smile on her face. Georgina bustles around with her chores and disappears inside to secretly watch the afternoon soapies.

"Where are you, Georgina?" Yannis calls.

"What do you want? I can get it," I said.

I cover for her when Yannis wants something; give him water, nibbles. If he discovers she is watching the soapies, he becomes very angry.

Every few days, I ring home. Alan updates me on the latest dramas in Australia.

Arthur, my husband's father with Alzheimer's disease, has fallen and broken his wrist. Clare, his wife, cannot deal with his Alzheimer's, much less the plaster on his wrist. Aunt Maisie is helping. Our children are fine.

I have taken to hiding the Nulax aperient medication from Mother. She is currently having eight to ten bowel actions day and night. She is obsessed with her bowels. She wants to open them every hour.

Put my foot down.

"It is not good for you to have so many bowel actions a day," I said.

"I haven't opened my bowels for a week," she said.

I show the soiled pants but does not convince her. Mother mutters that I am working with the devil.

She has developed leaky bowels and is always soiled. I wash piles of her clothes every day and make sure I hang them on the line in the proper manner.

Am sleep deprived with the endless toileting. Am too tired to argue with her, go for a short walk for sanity. When I return, find Mother rummaging through my things searching for the Nulax. She spends the rest of day muttering nasty things about me under her breath and putting me down in front of Aunt Georgina.

"My daughter put me into a nursing home," Mother said, her finger waggling in my direction.

"If your daughter must work, perhaps she had no other choice," said Georgina.

"I have not opened my bowels for a week," Mother said.

"You have opened your bowels four times already," I said.

Georgina pats Mother's hand and said, "Your daughter knows best."

Yannis is as demanding to Georgina as Mother is to me. Georgina and I are two refugees from the never-ending assault of caring.

~

One Friday, Mother, Georgina, and I take a taxi to the beach. Yannis is left at home with a friend. It is bliss. I love the sea, swim, the water cold and pleasant. There is no sand, only rocks. I swim to three fat ladies with enormous breasts who gossip and laugh. Mother and Georgina sit on the shore and talk.

~

One Wednesday, the neighbour Philomena from the wire fence takes Mother and me for a drive in her small car. She shows us the country place where she grows vegetables and fruit trees, takes us to her son-in-law's new home. It is elaborate, three stories high on a beautiful hill looking out to sea.

These memories of escape and happiness stand out in my memory.

CHAPTER 47

The trip continues

Cephalonia

July 1994

One morning, I am late returning from my morning walk by five minutes to find an agitated Georgina and a furious Mother.

"Where have you been? Your Mother has been calling for you," Georgina said.

I did not argue with her. She is under pressure. Yannis can be heard shouting in the background. Georgina, in turn, yells at me.

"Where do you go in the mornings?" said Mother, looking at me suspiciously.

"I know you are rounding up people to kill me; the voices told me," she hissed to me.

"I went for a swim," I said, holding up my wet bathers and wet hair.

She does not believe me.

Later in the day, Mother begs Yannis for his aperient Agarol. Unfortunately, he gives her some. Mother smirks at me, has four bowel actions in the day, and I clean soiled pants for days.

I loathe it all. Am tortured by Yannis, Georgina, and Mother.

~

One day, Georgina takes me aside and demands I stop my morning and afternoon walks.

"The neighbours think you are searching for a new husband," she said.

My eyes grow wide. I think fast.

"I am taking photos of the island for my husband Alan." I point to my camera in my bum bag.

"Alan asked me to take many photos to share with him on my return to Australia," I said.

I lie. Alan hates photos.

It is a plausible story in a land where the male is king. It is accepted. I breathe a sigh of relief. The explanation will be relayed to the gossipy neighbours.

I make sure wherever I walk, I wear my camera swung around my neck in full view. Make a big show of taking photos of houses trees, children, everything.

~

One day, when Yannis is in a particularly dark mood, he berates Mother for cutting off communication with the family.

"Our Mother cried every day, waiting for a letter from you. How could you have been so cruel, Ekaterini?" he asked.

Mother looks in the distance and does not answer.

"Our Mother called out 'Ekaterini my daughter, where are you?' just before she died," said Yannis.

Mother turns her head and looks out of the window. Still does not speak.

Try to explain about mental illness but do not have the proper words. They do not understand.

In Australia, Mother told me she stopped writing to her family after father died. Her Mother had written she intended to come to Australia and live permanently with us. We barely had enough to feed ourselves, much less a demanding old woman.

So many twists and turns in the stories.

Cannot even guess at the truthfulness of what I have been told.

~

Philomena from the wire fence suggests a treat for us. Takes Mother, Georgina, and me to Saint Gerasimos monastery. Again, Yannis stays behind and is looked after by a friend.

Georgina is bright, tells entertaining stories about places we pass, and gossips about people Philomena and she know. This is a lively Georgina, so different away from the stress of caring for Yannis.

The monastery is inundated with crowds of people. Mother smiles for the first time in ages; this must be a miracle. We light candles.

I pray for resilience and wisdom.

The church at Saint Gerasimos is ancient. The body of Saint Gerasimos is guarded and protected in a glass casement in a cave within the monastery. It is said that after his death, his body was buried twice and never decomposed. The church ordained him as a saint in 1622, and he is considered the patron saint of Cephalonia. The monastery is considered one of the most sacred pilgrimages in Cephalonia. The small church to Agios Gerasimos is built above the tomb and cave of the saint.

On our return, Yannis makes anti-religious jokes against the clergy.

~

Another night, after Yannis and Mother are in bed, Georgina lets out her frustration about Yannis. I have never seen her so enraged.

"The incompetent doctors have ruined Yannis's life and mine." She cried as if she couldn't stop, eventfully wiped her eyes on her apron and looked at me.

"I cannot bear to see him in agony all the time. I am trapped in Yannis's pain as he is."

"I am annoyed that I can't take you and your Mother out more because of Yannis."

I comfort her as best I can.

"We don't need outings. I do understand it is tough with Yannis, and us being here adds to your work."

"No, no, you don't understand, we love having you both here." She blows into her tissue.

"Our lives have changed so much since the botched operation. It is all pain and agony. But you and your Mother being here has made Yannis smile, and we have a reason for getting up in the morning."

~

The days merge. It is difficult to know when one starts and the other ends. Yannis smokes nonstop. He puffs all the time. I hate cigarette smoke at the best of times and loathe being surrounded by it. I have a headache from being in the room with his smoking. I cough and cough. No one mentions his smoking.

I have counted the days until we leave. Although I appreciate the generosity, it has been torture. I confirm our plane tickets.

On the final morning before our departure, I sit on a park bench, watch the sun rise over the sea. Church bells peel. It is lovely, but I have only seen such a small glimpse of the beauty of the island.

Neighbours came to see us off. Big kisses and hugs to all especially from Yannis and Georgina. Yannis sobs to see us leave, clings to Mother.

"I will never see you again," he said.

Mother pats him on the back but shows no emotion.

Goodbye Cephalonia and goodbye Aunt Georgina and Uncle Yannis.

I will never forget you, ever.

~

When we arrive in Athens, I succeed in hiring a taxi to the Stanley Hotel, no difficulty this time. Book in without incidence.

Athens bustles and never stops.

Mother and I watch the sunset over the Parthenon from the roof garden. The Stanley Hotel has been renovated since we were last here and seems classier. We enjoy a light beer. Again, enjoy the delicious cheese puffs Georgina gave us.

Wished I could have seen the Parthenon and seen a few of Athens' highlights.

But is impossible with Mother; she is old and tired and deep in her mental illness and paranoia about me.

"I know you bought me here to kill me," she hissed with venom in her voice.

I guess the voices told her.

She asks to go to bed.

I ring Taci and we speak for a long time.

"Please come and stay with me for a few days," he said. "Change your departure date."

"I have to go back to the university; my students will be waiting for me," I said.

I ring Renulla who wants us to fly over to Mytilene and stay with her for a while. I wish we could. I loved the delightful trip the previous year to Mytilene. In my mind, expected Cephalonia to be the same.

Next day, Gulf Air takes us back to Australia. The plane stops at Bahrain but not because of engine trouble this time.

Mother is jetlagged and confused. But has the energy to mutter horrible things about me, picks at her lips until they bleed.

Eventually, we arrive in Australia and Alan is there to meet us.

We are back.

PART 5

Mother dies

CHAPTER 48

Mother dies

Melbourne Jan / Feb 2009

During summer, when the heat is the most oppressive, Mother has her fourth heart attack and is admitted into Sunshine Hospital. She is medicated and discharged back to the Fronditha Greek Nursing for palliative care.

Nothing more can be done for her except pain relief. She is in heart failure and has a short time to live.

I notify my workplace, tell them I will be away for a few days.

Ring Alan, ask him to bring a change of clothes and my toilet bag.

My intention is to stay by Mother's side until she dies. Years ago, she asked me to be at her bedside and I promised to be there. The journey to the other side can be lonely without a loved one holding your hand.

The overhead fan in Mother's room creates a breeze, the curtains flutter.

"Mother is dying," I tell John and Jim in South Australia.

The words can barely come out of my mouth. I choke up. She is ninety-six years old, death is expected, but death always creates a shock. Even if expected.

John's family make plans to fly over. Jim is unable to come to Victoria as he is in the hospital himself, having treatment for leukaemia.

I gently place the phone to Mother's ear so she can speak to Jim. It will be the last time they will speak to each other. Jim is her *golden boy;* they have always had a symbiotic relationship. A spiritual connection between Jim and Mother. John and I have never been part of that. There is no bitterness, just an understanding, an acceptance of the facts.

Jim tries to speak, his words are whispers, it is very difficult for him. His own illness has been devastating, physically and emotionally.

"I love you Mother," he said.

I can hear him crying.

"I love you more," she said.

This has always been her stock answer to 'I love you' statements.

It feels surreal. I am not connected to the room.

The Fronditha staff push a large comfortable armchair into Mother's room for me, provide tea, food, and warm blankets.

"Cally, where are you?" Mother asks.

"I'm here," I said, squeezing her hand.

"Right here."

"I love you," I said.

"I love you more," she said.

She is in pain; morphine injections help. I hold the straw to her mouth; she sips a few gulps of water. Drifts in and out of consciousness.

Am motionless in the noiseless room, listening to her breathe.

A Greek priest gives the last rites. He comes in quietly and says prayers over her head, anointing her with oil. Mother opens her eyes as he speaks, stares briefly as if in disbelief, then closes them.

She is restless with the pain, the morphine increased.

"God bless you, Ekaterini, I will miss you," the Fronditha staff come in to say their goodbyes.

They leave tear-stained. She has been a favourite with the staff. They mention her lovely caring nature.

John, Helen, their daughter Barbara, and her sons Jordan and Blake arrive. They spend precious time with Mother. They tell her they love her. Mother is surrounded by people who love her.

By now she is unresponsive, breathes with difficulty.

Late at night, John and his family go to their hotel.

I stay by her bedside.

The room is a hallowed place.

There are spirits coming for Ekaterini to help her to the other side.

It will be her turn soon.

"I love you," I said.

"I am here with you."

Her breathing laboured, slower, and deeper.

The extended family smile from the many photos around Mother's room.

My children ring from overseas, say goodbyes to Mother. Each time I put the phone to her ears, I feel her body give a small jerk in a glimmer of recognition.

Mother stops breathing at 2.45 a.m., died on the second of February, the day of my daughter's birthday.

Her pain and suffering over, at peace.

She is free.

I want to believe she is in the arms of loved ones on the other side.

She had a difficult and tragic life, battled physical and mental illnesses.

Left a legacy of love, children and grandchildren and great-grandchildren.

Much of her past life has remained closed to me. Some secrets revealed during the trips to Greece and Cephalonia. But I never learnt the full story of her life, now I never will.

Who was my Mother?

The choices we make can lead us in different paths in life.

What sort of life would Mother have had if she had stayed in Lesvos?

What would have been different if Father had not died so young?

Would she have developed the mental illness which plagued her life? Despite the mental illness, she functioned and made the best of every situation. She loved deeply and was greatly loved back.

I sit motionless next to her body until dawn breaks.

Birds call to each other; two small sparrows pick at something on the grass. Open the door to the garden, feel the freshness flow into the room.

Goodbye Mother, I love you and will miss you.

PART 6

Seeing the world through older woman's eyes

Return to Mytilene , 2009

CHAPTER 49

Letting Mother's spirit free

Mytilene

October 2009

It is full circle, back to the start, back to the house, back to the harbour, back to the beginning.

Today in 2009, I gaze from The Blue Seas balcony as I did in 1993, when a joyous Mother returned to Lesvos.

Mother left Lesvos in 1952 with me as her daughter. This time, Alan, daughter Cath and her three-month daughter Ava, have returned. This is the first time Cath and Ava have been to Lesvos. We plan to retrace Mother's life and have a special memorial service for her in the island.

What did my Mother think when she bundled up her three children to leave this lovely place in 1952?

What went on in her mind as she packed her possessions, said goodbye to everything familiar and dear to her, for an uncertain future?

If she knew Father would be killed in a motor vehicle accident in Australia in 1956 and be left with no money nor supports to care for three children, she would never have left.

Did the family walk together from Thyra Street?

Did they have a taxi?

Did Mother have a long last look at her home?

She never wanted to leave her home or island.

What did my brothers feel?

I was too young to understand, perhaps excited to be going on a boat. Perhaps I gripped Mother's hand, not letting go.

The story of Mother needs to be told in the context of this magnificent island. She was a happy, popular woman with many friends and extended family. In Australia, she was disconnected, alienated, a foreigner, an outsider.

What secrets are still to be revealed about Father and Mother? Taci gave a few clues. Alcohol and friendliness opened his mouth to tell me things no one else could. But he is dead now.

This morning, watch the sky lighten, boats sway in the sea in front. The central point of the waterway is a small fort flying the blue-and-white Greek flag. Again, noise and activity build up at the harbour. Cars, trucks, bikes roar past. Trucks crunch gears.

Two little dogs bark excitedly at a man in the harbour. Are they guarding a boat? One dog, tail wagging, decides to follow the man. Watch two women carry their identical jackets with fur trim as they drag their suitcases with wheels to the ferry. A man in uniform strides past. The two little dogs decide to follow him. They appear to be marching together.

Motorcycles in bright colours roar past; the engines scream like mosquitoes. Music blares from a car.

A brown dog positions himself for a nap in the middle of the road. He is woken by cars honking, shakes, and ambles to the footpath.

I am smiling from ear to ear. I never expected to have the good fortune to return to Lesvos.

CHAPTER 50

The more things change the more they stay the same

Mytilene

November 2009

I notify Nassia and Nikos that we are back and organise a visit to Renulla and Michael's home. Tragically, Renulla now suffers from advanced Alzheimer's disease. This wonderful woman who was the central point of everything when we were here last is lost to Alzheimer's disease. Renulla is cared by her extended family. An Albanian woman is hired to look after her at night. Renulla has lost her memory, does not remember anyone. But she makes a fuss of baby Ava, who gurgles and laughs when held by Renulla.

Renulla's husband Michael looks on, eyes full of sadness.

Nassia and Nikos invite us to their home and assist us in our journey of remembrance as Renulla did in 1993. They arrange a special, extended family dinner with their family and their brother's family at a restaurant called The Eucalyptus. We talk until late. They make a special fuss over Cath and Ava. One of my wishes is fulfilled; Cath has had a chance to meet her wonderful Greek relatives in Lesvos.

Again, am elated by the sense of being in a wonderful extended family.

We find an English-speaking taxi driver. His name is Dennis, once lived in Sydney. He becomes personally involved in our search for relevant places from the past. He assists us to locate Mother's childhood home in Verga. He chooses a special fisherman's restaurant for lunch. There is no menu; only the fish catch of the day. The fish delicious and crispy, with fresh salads and vegetables.

The next day we manage to find the house in Verga, connect again with the aunt who was so generous to us in 1993. She points out the table under the walnut tree where we shared such happy times years ago. Her fruit trees magnificent, Michael still tends them as he did before.

The old family home in Thyra Street is now boarded up.

'For Sale' said the sign.

There is no sign of the old man and lovely sweet-faced woman who let us wander through the old home in 1993.

One neighbour who sees us loitering outside beckons us in for a coffee.

"You should buy the house," said a neighbour.

"I should," I said.

~

Show Cath and Ava the Castle, walk in the cool of the dark pine forest.

We become part of a noisy town festivity, celebrating the end of the German occupation of the island and World War II.

Friday, we take Mother's favourite blue scarf to the church of Saint Theodore. We light candles, say prayers.

I climb a large rock near the sea, hold up Mother's scarf, let the wind take the scarf into the sky and up above the sea. It rises higher and higher in the wind, dances above us before it sails away into the sky.

"May your spirit be free Mother," I said.

CHAPTER 51

2017 Postscript

Mother and Father are both dead. Brother Jim and John are gone, both died from cancer. I am the sole survivor of our small family. This Memoir has been written so my brothers' families and mine will remember Ekaterini and Michael Evangelou.

~

Mother

Mother was born on 24th April 1912 in Mytilene, Lesvos and died in Melbourne 2nd February 2009. She died the year tragic bushfires swept through Victoria killing many people.

She loved her husband Michael and her three children John, Jim, and me. She adored her daughter-in-law Helen and son-in-law-Alan, loved her grandchildren and great-grandchildren. She, in turn, was cherished by them.

Mother did not leave money or an estate, had no fine jewellery, but her legacy was more valuable than any possessions. My inheritance from Mother was she taught me to be resilient. To get on with whatever is handed to you in life and make the best of it. Not to complain.

During the Second World War, Father enlisted in the Greek Army and was placed in the Greek Medical Corp. He was in Albania when German troops invaded Lesvos. Mother recalled the extreme hardship of the Greek people during the German occupation. Locals were rounded up by the Germans and punished severely for any infringement of rules. Other Greeks were shot or hung from trees by fellow Greeks for collaborating with the Germans. It was a time of fear and trepidation.

Mother recounted harrowing tales about women she knew. Some women had to prostitute themselves to the German troops to obtain money to feed their children. Poverty, hunger, disease was everywhere. Mother at the time was a young woman not yet twenty-one and my brother John a baby. She had not heard from Father in months, not knowing if he had been killed or still alive. My Grandmother stayed in the house with Mother and together they grew vegetables, milked a goat for milk, and survived.

After the war, life improved.

When I was a child, we enjoyed a contented life in Mytilene. Lived in a pleasant home near friends and relatives. Father worked for a good company.

Mother was popular with those around her. John and Jim did well in school, even learning the violin.

This changed in 1952 when Father decided to migrate to Australia. Mother argued and fought the move. She did not want to leave the island. Father would not change his mind. He sold the house and its contents, paid for our tickets to Australia. One of Father's contacts in Australia told tales of Australia as a country of great opportunity.

Mother left everything meaningful to her in Lesvos; friends, mother and brother, home, position in society. On arrival in Australia, the stark reality contrasted vastly from the positive image my Father's friend had espoused. We were poor; Father's accountancy qualifications were not accepted. Australia at the time only wanted factory workers and pushed migrants into factory work and closed off other avenues of employment.

From being the popular woman in Mytilene, she became an isolated Greek woman who could not speak English. Mother told about the difficulties in communication at a Springvale grocers shop; she wanted 'cheese,' and couldn't remember the word and struggled.

The shop woman laughed at her and said, "speak English."

~

I remember Mother in continuous motion; sewing, cooking gardening, learning new things. I never knew until years later, when I taped a narrative of her story, how desperately homesick she was, cried in private.

Mother saw greatness in her three children. She encouraged us with our school work and gave us the impression we were more marvellous than we were and could achieve most things.

I remember coming home from school with a report card of all A's and one B and being told sternly if I tried harder, I might be an A student in all subjects. She tried to help me with my schoolwork, although she could only read simple English. One time, she took an English correspondence course to improve her English, so she could help me with my spelling tests.

Through Mother, I learnt that there are things that defy understanding and have extraordinary meaning.

Years later, my mother-in-law Clare's dementia increased along with her physical health deteriorated. She was admitted into Footscray Society of the Aged Nursing Home.

Mother lived in a Greek nursing home when her physical and mental state worsened. Mother insisted that I collect her and visit Clare every Sunday. We would arrive at Clare's nursing home. Clare recognised Mother, even if she did not recognise her sons.

Mother called Clare "Mrs Berryman" and Clare called Mother "Mrs E."

My Mother had disengaged from English and only spoke in Greek, as is common in elderly people from other countries; they revert to the language of origin.

Mother chattered in Greek to Clare, and Clare babbled in her jumble of nonsensical English words. They would communicate like this for the afternoon visit. I would provide a lavish afternoon tea. When it became time to go, Clare would ask Mrs E to come again and Mother solemnly promised she would.

~

Father

When I was a young child, Father brought my brothers and me comics each payday. I would receive a Jack and Jill comic, my brothers Superman and Phantom.

"We haven't the money for frivolous things like comics," Mother said.

"The children need some fun," he said. "The comics encourage reading."

Despite her protests, the comics would be sitting on the dressing table when we woke up. Both my brothers and I loved the comics and after reading them many times would swap them with friends when finished.

Father's garden had been his joy. He planted rows of vegetables; we shared excess with neighbours.

When I turned eight, Father organised my first real birthday party with our family and two school friends. For the first time in my life, we played party games. I received the Mama doll and remember carrying it carefully in its box from the shop to home. I still have the doll.

Father encouraged us to join the Church of England. He invited priests home for lunch as he felt sorry for them not having a home. They would discuss deep philosophical issues over the meal. Mother grumbled as barely had enough to feed us, much less priests. Father saw it as an honour.

Immigration to Australia meant unemployment for my Father. He eventually he found a factory job at the Fisherman's Bend branch of General Motors Holden. The shift work was dirty—noisy, dangerous, and difficult for a man who had been an accountant and used his brains to earn a living. In Australia during those years, migrants were only used as a conduit for filthy factory work that other Australians refused. To update Father's Greek qualifications to Australian requirements was costly and difficult.

At one stage, Father sustained damage to his hand; it caught in the factory machinery. Crying with pain, his hand bound up, he would still go to work. We had a mortgage, no furniture, slept on the floor covered in blankets. Eventually, beds and table and chairs were bought on hire purchase. Father found a better job at the Post Office sorting letters. It helped him learn the names of the suburbs.

The shift work killed him. Coming home late, he was hit by a car and died three days later at The Alfred Hospital.

There was no compensation in those days. No Transport Accident Commission.

Mother was ignorant of the law, even having to pay the Alfred hospital fees. The neighbours raised a little money to help us pay for the funeral and urgent bills. Father's death created a downward spiral that brought the family to its knees. John and Jim had to have special permission to leave school in their teens. Mother cooked, cleaned, worked in the garden, sewed for neighbours, and went crazy in her grief.

To have been forced to come to Australia against her will had been bad enough, but now in a strange land, a widow and poor. It was too much.

www.ingramcontent.com/pod-product-compliance
Lightning Source LLC
Chambersburg PA
CBHW022135020426
42334CB00015B/910

* 9 7 8 0 6 4 8 2 8 5 1 0 6 *